Foul Football

THE FAMOUSLY FOUL FOOTBALL BOOK

Michael Coleman

SCHOLASTIC

Scholastic Children's Books
Euston House, 24 Eversholt Street
London, NW1 1DB

A division of Scholastic Ltd
London ~ New York ~ Toronto ~ Sydney ~ Auckland
Mexico City ~ New Delhi ~ Hong Kong

The Bootiful Game
First published in the UK as Foul Football by Scholastic Ltd, 1997
Text copyright © Michael Coleman, 1997
Illustrations copyright © Harry Venning, 1997

The Bootiful Game: Second Half
First published in the UK as Even Fouler Football by Scholastic Ltd, 2004
Text copyright © Michael Coleman, 2004
Illustrations copyright © Mike Phillips, 2004

This compilation copyright © Scholastic Ltd, 2009

Some of the material in this book has previously been published in
Foul Football: Great Big Quiz Book
First published in the UK by Scholastic Ltd, 2001
Text copyright © Michael Coleman, 2001
Illustrations © by Mike Phillips, 2001

CONTENTS

Foul Football

The Bootiful Game

First Half

CONTENTS

INTRODUCTION

Are you a foul footballer? Of course you aren't, otherwise you'd be kicking this book instead of reading it! No, I bet you're somebody who simply enjoys playing the best, the most exciting, game in the world.

So, what do you like best about playing football?

- scoring loads of great goals?
- getting in plenty of terrific tackles?
- scaring the other team with some dreamy dribbling (not the messy sort!)?
- walloping fearsome free-kicks?
- being stamped on, beaten up and generally hacked to bits?

Well, unless you enjoy playing against really foul teams (a team of teachers, for instance) then you probably didn't pick the last option!

If you'd been playing football when the game first began, though, that would definitely have been your choice – because that was what football was all about. There were very few rules. Stamping, hacking, and generally beating up the players on the other side was all part of the game.

It's a wonder the game didn't end up being called foot-brawl instead of football!

What's more, if you didn't end up in hospital you could end up in jail. Football was often banned because it was so rough. It's said that King Richard II stopped his soldiers playing a game of football – because he was afraid they'd all be too crocked to fight the French army!

Nowadays things are a bit different. Football is played the world over, by boys and girls, men and women. It's a great game, full of skill. There are strict rules, and the best footballers are those that everybody else is frightened of playing against because they're so good, not because they're big and mean and ugly (unless they play for a team of teachers…).

Of course, this doesn't mean that you won't meet some pretty foul footballers in this book. You certainly will!

You'll meet:
- foul footballers and fair footballers
- fair teams and foul teams … and their foul managers!

You'll read about:
- some fair trophy-winners…
- and some foul flops!

And you'll even discover some frightening facts about:
- foul referees!
- and foul fans!

Added to all this, you'll discover the winners of our unique **Foul Football Awards** – such as:

THE FOULEST FOUL
FOOTBALLERS AWARD…
Patrick Viera (Arsenal) and Duncan Ferguson (Everton) who share the record of being sent off 8 times in the Premier League.

So start reading … but if you're reading in class, watch out for your teacher. You don't want to get fouled!

FOUL FOOTBALL

There is a legend that English football began in the 8th century. The Saxons and the Vikings had just had a big battle (the first international match!) which the Saxons had won. The beaten Viking squad had gone away empty-handed. Worse, at least one of them had ended up empty-shouldered as well – a Saxon had cut off his head as a souvenir!

But what can you do with a spare head?

At which point they all looked at each other and shouted: "Yeh! That's what we'll do with it!"

And so they did – they used the Viking's head as a football!

Putting the boot in

However the game really started, "foot-balle" (as it was known) was certainly played in medieval times. A real foul game it was, too! You wouldn't have persuaded King Edward III to give out the medals at the Cup Final – in the 14th century he issued a proclamation banning the game:

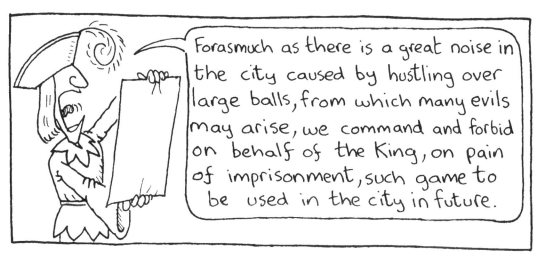

Forasmuch as there is a great noise in the city caused by hustling over large balls, from which many evils may arise, we command and forbid on behalf of the King, on pain of imprisonment, such game to be used in the city in future.

But over two hundred years later the game was still being played – and, if anything, it had become even fouler! Philip Stubbes was a Puritan who wrote, in 1583, about the nasty goings-on that he thought needed to be stamped out:

As concerning footballe playing, I protest unto you that it may be called a friendlie kind of fight....

In 1829 a big game took place in Derbyshire. The match report talked of many players:

"...falling, bleeding beneath the feet of the surrounding mob."

Sounds more like a game in your school playground, doesn't it?

But, in spite of all this, the game survived. Even though Kings may not have liked it, the peasants did.

They'd play it on Sundays – presumably because, after being down-trodden by their masters all week, it gave them a chance to do some down-treading of their own.

A game called "hurling at goales" was popular in Cornwall in the 16th and 17th centuries and, in the 17th and 18th centuries a game called 'kicking camp' was played in East Anglia (bad news if your name was Camp!).

These games were between neighbouring villages. They would often play each other on a special day, just once a year – probably because it took them that long to recover!

Did you know?
A favourite day for playing foot-balle was Shrove Tuesday, the day we still call "pancake day".
Maybe this was because a lot of the players ended the game as flat as one!

Perhaps you'd like to try setting up a school foot-balle match of your own. Here's how to do it:

Find a pig.

Remove its bladder (don't forget to ask pig's permission).

Pump it up (the bladder, not the pig) and tie a knot in the end. You've now got your balle.

Pick your school team. This is easy. Everybody can play! (Forget 11-a-side. For a good game of foot-balle you want at least 150-a-side!!)

Send out a challenge to the school down the road.

Find a pitch to play on. The road between your school and theirs is perfect.

At the start of the game your team goes to the end of the road and their team to the other.

Somebody throws the balle into the middle of the road — and then both teams.....

CHARGE!

The aim of the game is to score goals, of course. Your team is aiming to get the ball into the other school's goal which is at their end of the road. How you get it there doesn't matter. You can kick it, pick it up and throw it, pick up the person who's got the ball and throw them… The referee won't stop you, for the simple reason that there isn't one – who needs a ref when there aren't any rules?

Foul football rules

Rules arrived in the middle of the 19th century. By then, football was a popular game at public schools, like Eton and Harrow. What they'd done, though, was to take the foul village punch-up kind of football and turn it into a sport with some rules.

The problem, though, was that each school devised their own rules. This made life pretty tricky when they wanted to play against each other. (If you're not sure why, try to imagine playing a school football match against a team who think you're playing rugby!) So, in 1848, after a couple of false starts, the first set of rules was adopted.

They were known as the 'Cambridge Rules' because they were first tried out in a game at Cambridge University.

Cambridge Rules, O.K.?

Try this tricky ten quiz. Were each of the following in the Cambridge Rules – YES or NO?

1. The pitch could be up to 200 yards (183m) long x 100 yards (91m) wide – YES/NO
2. The goalposts could be as high as you liked – YES/NO
3. To score a goal the ball had to be kicked between the posts – YES/NO
4. Teams changed ends every time a goal was scored – YES/NO
5. When the ball went off at the side of the pitch it had to be thrown in again. No player was allowed to touch the ball until it hit the ground – YES/NO
6. If one of the other team kicked the ball behind your goal then your team got a goal-kick, but if one of your players touched it last the other team got a free

kick! – YES/NO

7. Any player could catch the ball, but not run with it – YES/NO

8. Picking the ball up, or passing it with the hands, was forbidden – YES/NO

9. The ball could only be passed backwards, not forwards – YES/NO

10. You couldn't trip, hack, hold or push … and you weren't allowed to wear boots with nails sticking out of the bottom – YES/NO

Answers: YES! They were ALL in the Cambridge Rules!

1. Nowadays the pitch can't be bigger than 130 yards x 100 yards (120m x 91m).
2. There was no limit to the height of the goal! Great for hoofers!
3. Crossbars weren't invented until much later.
4. Pretty boring if the score was 50-0!
5. And throw-ins had to be taken one-handed!
6. the penalty was actually called a free kick and had to be taken in line with wherever the ball went out.
7. After catching the ball, you could make a mark on the pitch with your heel; you were then awarded a free-kick.
8. You could only pass the ball by kicking it.
9. If you were in front of the ball you were "offside". You weren't allowed to touch the ball or tackle anybody.
10. You weren't allowed iron plates on the bottom of your boots either!

As you can see, football played by the Cambridge Rules was pretty different to the game we know now. It was much more like rugby. In fact rules 2, 3, 5 and 9 are still in the game of rugby as it's played today.

Football rulers – The Football Association

The Football Association (or F.A. as it is usually known) was formed in 1863 by a number of football clubs in the London area. The idea was that the F.A. would publish a set of agreed football rules, and these would be the rules used when any of the F.A.'s member clubs played each other.

Starting with the Cambridge Rules, the clubs had a meeting … and another meeting … and another…

This was the moment when Rugby and Association Football parted company. The 'hacking' fans left to begin the Rugby Union, leaving the remaining F.A. members to set about developing the game we know today.

16

> **Foul football question:**
> What word does "soccer" come from?
> Answer:
> From the word "asSOCiation".
> It was supposedly invented in 1889 by a man named Charles Wreford-Brown who, when asked if he wanted to play rugger (rugby) replied, "No, I'm going for a game of soccer".

Fair women and foul officials

Once the game started to get a bit organized, women decided they'd play it too.

Unfortunately, that's when they ran into some foul officials!

The British Ladies Football Club was formed in the 1890s by the perfectly-named Nettie Honeyball. A crowd of 10,000 turned out to watch their first game! The trouble was, some of the crowd were officials of the F.A. who described the game as "a farce". They thought football was a man's game, and that the whole idea of women playing football was daft.

In 1902, they banned all their member teams from playing against women's teams and, in 1921, even went as far as to ban them from playing games on the grounds of league teams.

They were probably jealous. A very well-known team, formed in 1894, was called Dick Kerr's Ladies. They toured the country (they even went to America) playing games to raise money for charity. In 1917, in the middle of the First World War, they'd even played

17

at Goodison Park, home of Everton, to raise money for a military hospital.

How big was the crowd for that game?

a) 15,000

b) 20,000

c) 25,000

It wasn't until over 50 years later, in 1969, that the Football Association finally recognized that girls and women had a right to play football too. Now there's a Women's F.A., hundreds of women's football clubs, and a full programme of national and international competitions.

But it's not all good news. The F.A. still won't let women's teams play against men's teams. They won't even let girls play in the same team as team as boys once they're over 12 years old! Maybe they're worried that the girls will be better? Whatever the reason, they'll have to change their mind one day. In the meantime, girls, keep on playing the game. And no fouling!

Foul football quote

"I'd kick my own brother if necessary. That's what being a professional is all about."
Steve McMahon, Liverpool & England.

No fouls! The laws of football timeline

The rules, or laws, of football have often changed – usually to stop some foul footballer who'd thought of a sneaky way of getting round them! Here's how…

1863 To stop games ending up 75-all, the goals were reduced from as-high-as-you-liked to 20ft high This was done by simply stretching a tape between the posts.

1871 The size and weight of the ball was fixed. Its circumference had to be somewhere between 8.5cm and 71cm, and it had to weigh between 397g and 454g. So, no Viking heads!

1871 Goalkeepers were mentioned in the rules for the first time. Until this date everybody was allowed to catch the ball – so everybody was a goalkeeper! Now, only a team's goalkeeper could catch the ball. Who was the goalkeeper? The player nearest the goal – so everybody was still a goalkeeper!

1872 Instead of giving away a free kick when you put the ball behind your goal, corner kicks were invented instead.

1877 With a tape crossbar nobody knew if a goal really had been scored. To get round this a solid crossbar was introduced and its height fixed at 8 ft (2.4 m)

1883 Throw-ins now had to be taken two-handed; up until now they'd been taken one-handed.

1891 Goal nets were introduced to help referees decide if the ball had gone between the posts.

1890 – 1892 Perilous penalties!

Of all the rule changes, those that have kicked up most fuss have been to do with penalty kicks.

This is what happened in the 1891 F.A. Cup quarter final between Notts County and Stoke…

Sorry, penalties weren't invented at that time. All poor old Stoke got was a free-kick which the Notts County goalkeeper easily smothered. (The rule making him stand ten yards away didn't exist either, remember!)

After this, in 1891, penalties – and penalty areas – were invented. Even then, some F.A. members objected. They thought a penalty law suggested that some of their players were ungentlemanly … which they were, of course!

Then, the next season, this happened in the match between Aston Villa and Stoke…

As the referee gave the penalty, Aston Villa's goalkeeper promptly picked the ball up and booted it out of the ground. By the time they'd got it back, time was up and Villa were the winners. After this, the rule was changed to allow extra time to be added on so that a penalty could be taken. As if that wasn't enough, another change came in 1892. Why? Because this was how you could take penalties at that time…

Bloggs runs in to take the penalty. Here he comes... Hello, what's he doing? He's dribbling the ball forward!....He's taking it closer to the goal! Wallop!! Yep, he's scored.....

Yes, it didn't have to be a penalty kick – it could be a penalty dribble! This made scoring penalties so easy that the rule was changed once again, this time to say that the penalty taker could only touch the ball once.

1912 Until now, goal-keepers had been allowed to handle the ball anywhere in their own half! This meant they could catch the ball near the halfway line and then try to belt it back into the other team's goal! After both goalkeepers had done this in one match the rule was changed to stop them handling the ball outside their own penalty area.

Only catch it in the Penalty area? I think I'll go back to playing cricket!

1913 Getting a free-kick wasn't a lot of use sometimes because the laws allowed the other team to stand just 6 yards (about 5 metres) from the ball! Now a rule was brought in to make them stand at least

Actually, lads, you're supposed to stand the other side.

ten yards (over 9m) away.

1914 The ten-yard rule was extended to cover corner kicks as well.

1924 Goals could be scored from corners.

1925 Somebody cut a corner! Everton beat Tottenham 1-0 after their winger Sam Chedgozy took a corner by dribbling the ball forward and then whacking it into the net! The rule was changed to say that the kicker could only touch the ball once.

1925 The 'orrible off-side rule was changed as well. This said that, when a player has passed the ball, at least three of the other team had to be between him and their goal. If they weren't then the player was offside and a free-kick was given. Defenders loved it! They'd become so good at "trapping" forwards offside that some matches were all free-kicks and no decent kicks. In 1925 the rule was changed to two defenders.

And now the forwards loved it! On the first day under the new rule, Aston Villa scored 10 against Burnley!

1929 When facing a penalty, goalkeepers weren't allowed to move before the ball was kicked.

1937 Defenders weren't allowed to tap the ball into their goalie's hands from a goal kick.

1981 The International F.A., F.I.F.A., accused footballers of becoming plonkers when they said that there was too much kissing going on. No law was brought in to stop it, though.

1992 Goalkeepers are not allowed to handle back-passes.

Foul football question:
When were kick-ins used instead of throw-ins?
Answer:
1993! An international trial was carried out. In England, the clubs in the semi-professional I.C.I.S. League had to play by this rule.

1996 Players who take their shirts off when celebrating a goal had to be given a yellow card.

THE SHIRTIEST PLAYER AWARD...
Steve Brown (Wycombe Wanderers) - When his club scored a last-minute winner to go into the FA Cup semi-final, Brown tore off his blue striped shirt in joy – only to see red. The yellow card he got was his second of the match, so the referee had to send him off.

2007 You can't lift your shirt over your head to celebrate a goal. Nor can you lift your shirt if there's a rude message or advertising underneath it.

2008 The rule-makers, The International FA (FIFA) show that the rules don't apply to them. They order that all official footballs have to carry a large 'FIFA' logo.

So that's how the rules have developed since 1863. Today, football is the most popular game in the world and many footballers have become celebrities – some of them foul celebrities!

Come on, then. Lace up your boots. Check your studs. We're off up the players' tunnel and on to the pitch. Let's see who we meet!

FOUL FOOTBALLERS

What makes a footballer?

Thousands of footballers have thrilled crowds since the game began. So, if you're going to become a footballer, what do you need to worry about?

Age anguish

Young or old, you can be a footballer. Scottish goalkeeper Ronnie Simpson (Queens Park, 1945) played his first game at the age of 14 years, 304 days! Alan Shearer (Southampton, 1988) became the youngest player to score a 1st Division hat-trick when he banged in three goals against Arsenal at the tender age of 17 years 240 days. And as for being too old, the legendary Stanley Matthews (Stoke, 1965) played his last game at the age of 50 years, 5 days!

Foul football question:
On the last day of the 1950/51 season, Alec Herd watched his 17 year-old son David play for Stockport. At the  same time, David watched his 39 year-old dad Alec play against Hartlepool. How did they manage it?
Answer:
Father and son were both playing for Stockport v Hartlepool!

How tall?

It doesn't matter how tall you are, either!

You can be very tall, like goalkeeper Albert Iremonger

(Notts County, 1900s) who was 1.98m, 4cm taller than the current England goalkeeper David James (Portsmouth). What's more, if anything annoyed Iremonger during a game he'd just sit on the ball in the middle of the field and, until things were put right, nobody could get him off it! In other words, Iremonger didn't bawl and shout, he balled and sat! On the other foot, you can be pretty short, like Alex James (Arsenal, 1930s). When he played against Walsall in the F.A. Cup, there

was a hole in the changing room wall, which the Walsall players peeped through. They saw that James had to stand on the bench to reach his changing room peg!

How heavy?

It doesn't even matter how heavy you are.

The enormous goalie "Fatty" Foulke (Sheffield Utd, 1890s and 1900s) weighed over 140kg. Next to him, Petr Cech (Chelsea) at 87kg would have looked like Petr the Puny! Foulke was an amazing character. His goal kicks sailed to the other penalty area, and he could punch the ball to the halfway line. And how do you think he dealt with foul forwards who annoyed him? He picked them up and dangled them by their ankles!

At the other end of the scales, the famous Irish footballer, Patsy Gallagher (Celtic and Northern Ireland, 1910-20s) weighed in at a mere 45kg – not much more than a cow-patsy! Compare him to Wayne Rooney at 79kg and Theo Walcott at 68kg.

Foul football question:
Patsy Gallagher once scored a remarkable goal for Celtic. He was lying on the goal-line, facing the wrong way, and with the ball trapped between his feet. So, how did he score?

Answer:
Still holding the ball between his feet, he did a back-somersault and landed in the goal!

So, what is important if you want to become a footballer? That depends on which position you want to play. Here are some foul examples to help you along!

Gruesome goalkeepers

As goalie you're the last line of defence. Your job is to stop the ball going between the posts (does that make you a postman as well as a footballer?). You can pick the ball up, but only in your penalty area.

So, you need…

- A sticky pair of hands – but not too sticky, like those of Gary Sprake (Leeds and Wales, 1960s and 1970s). In a game against Liverpool the ball stuck to his fingers as he went to throw it out – and he ended up throwing it into his own net instead.

- Not to mind getting dirty – unlike the Spanish international goalkeeper, Zamora. He played in the 1920s and 1930s, and hated dirt and mud so much that he'd occasionally keep a broom with him and tidy up the goalmouth! Perhaps he thought he was playing sweeper instead?

- Watch the game at all times – unlike Joachim Isadore. Playing for a Brazilian team called the Corinthians against Rio Preto, he let in the fastest goal in history – after just one second! Isadore had been saying some prayers and didn't realize the game had started.

Deadly defenders and marauding midfielders

Your job is to stop the other team's attacks and, if you can, join in with your own team's attacks. It's also great if you can score a few goals. But that means that you need...

- A good sense of direction – unlike Sammy Wynne (Man Utd, 1923), who seemed to get pretty confused when his team drew 2-2 against Oldham. Sammy scored all the goals – a penalty and a free-kick at the right end, and two own-goals at the wrong end!

- Good hearing – in particular, to know what the referee's whistle sounds like. Left-back Dennis Evans (Arsenal, 1955) heard a whistle and thought it was the ref blowing for the end of their match against Blackpool. So what did he do? Boot the ball into his own goal, only to discover that it counted. He'd scored an own goal! The whistle he'd heard had been blown by somebody in the crowd. Good job Arsenal were winning 4-0 at the time!

Amazing attackers

If you're an attacker, your job is simple. You've got to bang in the goals. That means some talents are very useful to you...

- A big head – like Peter Aldis (Aston Villa, 1952) against Sunderland, when he headed a goal from the record distance of 32 metres – the only goal he scored in his career!

- Be able to score in your sleep – like Nat Lofthouse (Bolton, 1950s). Playing for England against Austria, he collided with their 'keeper, but still managed to kick the ball. He was unconscious when it went into the net!

- Ball control – like Robert Vidal (Oxford University, 1873) whose nickname was 'The Prince of Dribblers'. In those days, the rule was that the team that scored also kicked off afterwards. On one occasion this rule allowed Vidal to score three goals in a match without the other team touching the ball!

THE 'MUST-IMPROVE-OUR-WRITING' AWARD...

Wolverhampton Wanderers – who were so famous in 1939 that their FA Cup Final opponents, Portsmouth, asked for their autographs! But when the Portsmouth players discovered that the writing was so bad they couldn't read them, they decided the Wolves team were just a bunch of bozos. No longer nervous, they went out and ripped Wolves apart, 4-1!

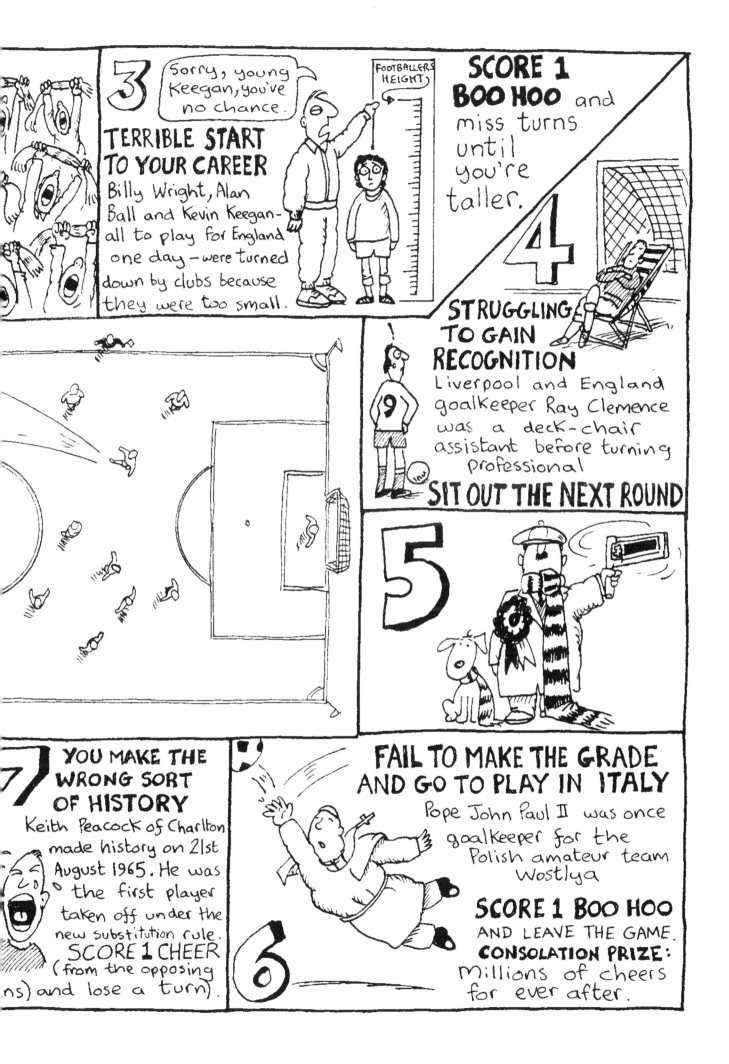

Foul fantasy football team

Maybe you'll end up being a star player just because you've got a good name. Here's a whole team full of the foulest names in foul football history!

Ron BATTY
Newcastle (1945-58)

Eddie BOOT
Huddersfield (1937-52)

Terry BUTCHER
Ipswich (1976-86)

Jesse CARVER
Blackburn (1925-35)

Walter CROOK
Blackburn (1932-47)

Bill DODGIN
Arsenal (1952-61)

Barry FRY
Man. United (1962-64)

Leslie GORE
Fulham (1933-36)

John HACKING
Oldham (1926-34)

Peter MADDEN
Rotherham (1955-66)

Joseph MALLETT
Southampton (1947-53)

MANAGER:
Ian ST. JOHN
Portsmouth (1974-77)

Foul injuries

If you're a footballer, there's always the chance of getting injured. If you're a foul footballer there's an even better chance of course, because somebody will probably want to foul you back! So, don't be surprised if your mum's really worried.

One mum who did get worried was that of Lord Arthur Kinnaird. Kinnaird played in the 1880s for both the Wanderers and the Old Etonians. He appeared in nine F.A. Cup Finals and won five winner's medals, but his biggest claim to fame was his fearsome "hacking". It's said that another player, Lord Marindin, called on Kinnaird's mum one day.

MUM: He's playing that nasty football game again. I'm frightened that one day he'll come back with a broken leg.

MARINDIN: Don't worry, Mrs Kinnaird. It won't be his own!

THE HEAD-BANGER AWARD...

Norman Hunter (Leeds United) – who, after kicking Coventry's David Cross in the head, shouted: 'Good job I hit you in the head, Crossie, or I might have hurt you!' Mind you, head-banging wasn't usual for the Leeds hard man. His nickname was Norman 'Bites Yer Legs' Hunter!

Sadly, it's not unknown for players to actually die during the game – a pretty foul way to end your career.

Goalkeepers seem to be in danger the most, usually when they rush out and dive at somebody's feet. John Thomson (Celtic, 1931) did this in a match against Rangers and died from a fractured skull. Maybe goalies should wear safety helmets like cricketers do nowadays?

Bob Benson (Arsenal, 1913) made a tragic decision, too. He'd been retired for a year after a playing career with Sheffield Utd, when he was persuaded to make a comeback with Arsenal. In the middle of his first game, against Reading, he felt ill and went off. He died in the changing room.

Thankfully, not all injuries are as bad as these. Most only result in broken bones and twisted bits! So, if you're going to be a foul footballer it's a good idea to know something about anatomy. That way you'll be able to tell the doctor which bone you've broken or bit you've twisted!

Battered bones

Try this quiz about players who've broken bones. It's a real cracker!

a) Goalkeeper Jim Blyth (Birmingham, 1982) played for over an hour in a match against Sunderland with a broken what?

b) What did Gerry Byrne (Liverpool, 1965) break after five minutes of the F.A. Cup Final against Leeds?

c) Dave Mackay (Tottenham, 1964) broke this when playing for Tottenham Hotspur, spent nine months recovering, then broke it again in his comeback match!

d) What did Bert Trautmann (Man City, 1956) break 15 minutes from the end of the F.A. Cup Final against Birmingham?

e) When Chelsea goalkeeper Petr Cech collided with Reading's Stephen Hunt in 2006 he broke his – what?

Answers:

a) Right arm – broken in three places!

b) Collar bone. He played out the remaining 85mins … and then 30 mins of extra time!

c) Left leg. It didn't stop him though. Mackay went on to win the F.A. Cup with Spurs and the Second Division championship with Derby County

d) Neck! He played on, though – and went up to get his medal!

e) His skull! Cech now has a metal plate in his head and plays wearing a padded cap. Now you know why they say that goalkeepers are a bit cracked!

Finally, there was the case of 19 year-old Frank Swift (Manchester City, 1934) who collapsed at the end of the F.A. Cup Final against Portsmouth. He hadn't broken anything, though. He'd simply fainted!

Foul football boots

Surprisingly enough, footballers don't wear much in the way of protection. The only hard bits (apart from their heads) are the boots on their feet and the shinpads on their legs.

Shinpads, or shinguards as they were called, were originally worn outside your socks! They were made out of strips of cane, encased in leather. They looked a bit like a small pair of cricket pads.

Shinguards worn inside the socks were invented in 1874. A man named Sam Widdowson invented them for himself. Why? Have a look at what football boots were

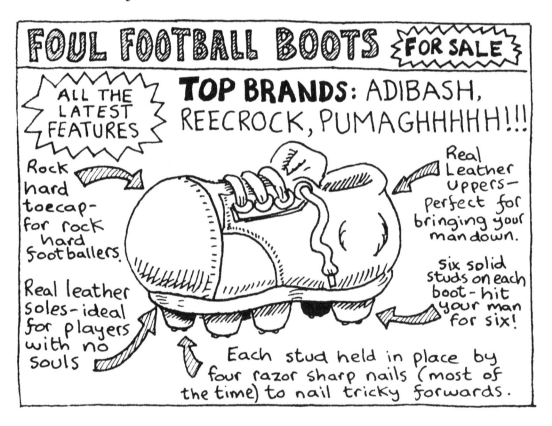

Pretty foul, eh? And until the 1960s that's the sort you'd have had to wear! That's when the lightweight boots we see nowadays, with either screw-in studs or moulded soles, were invented. They make ball-control much easier – and tricky-winger-control much harder!

Freak fouls: crazy injuries

Not all injuries are the result of being kicked, though.
Some footballers have been injured in very curious ways.
Try this foul quiz…

1. Liam Lawrence (Stoke City, 2008) injured his ankle in a
   tackle with: a) the referee b) a dog c) a spectator
   a) the referee
   b) a small dog
   c) a spectator

2. England goalkeeper Chris Woods (1990) was trying to
   undo his track suit trousers when:
   a) he stabbed himself with a penknife
   b) the elastic snapped and broke his finger
   c) a button flew up and hit him in the eye

3. Steve Morrow (Arsenal, 1993) scored the winner for
   his team in the League Cup Final and then had his
   arm broken by:
   a) running into a goalpost
   b) being congratulated
   c) doing a somersault

4. Derek McInnes (West Bromwich Albion, 2002) injured his foot when:

a) his wife ran over it in the car
b) he kicked angrily at a flat tyre on his Ferrari
c) he ran into a traffic cone.

Answers:

1. b) He got up in the night, trod on his pet Labrador, and fell down the stairs.

2. a) He was really cut up about it, he had to miss the next England game.

3. b) And it was done by his own captain, Tony Adams. At the end of the game the delighted Adams hoisted Morrow over his shoulder – and dropped him! Morrow's injury meant he had to miss the F.A. Cup Final four weeks later.

4. c) The players used traffic cones to dodge between in training – but dopey Derek's dodging was dodgy and he didn't dodge!

Stanley Matthews – the wizard of the dribble

Stanley Matthews played top-class football for an amazing 33 years. He was born in 1915 and played his first game for his home-town club, Stoke City, when he was 17.

Matthews was a right-winger. This was his favourite trick. Try it in your next match.

It sounds very simple, but Stanley Matthews was so good at it that the trick worked brilliantly nearly every time. And when it came to running, he was so fast the full-back never, ever caught up with him.

Two years after playing his first game for Stoke, Matthews was picked for England. In all, he played for his country 54 times.

Stanley Matthews was incredibly popular. In 1938 he had a disagreement with the Stoke manager and asked for a transfer to another club. What happened? Three thousand fans held a protest meeting, with another 1000 locked outside the packed hall. It worked. The problems were sorted out, and Matthews stayed at Stoke until 1947. Then – in spite of another protest meeting – he was transferred to Blackpool for £11,500.

A year later, and at the age of 33, Stanley Matthews was voted Footballer of the Year, and played at Wembley in his first F.A. Cup Final. In a great game, Blackpool were beaten 2-4 by Manchester United. Three years later, in 1951, Blackpool reached the final again – and again Stanley Matthews picked up a loser's medal as his team lost 0-2 to Newcastle.

Would he ever get a winner's medal? In 1953, he had a third chance as Blackpool got to the Cup Final once more, to face Bolton Wanderers. At the age of 38, everybody said this would be his last chance.

And, with just over 20 minutes to go, it looked as though that chance had gone. Blackpool were losing 1-3. Then, they pulled a goal back … and Matthews started to weave his magic. With three minutes to go, Blackpool equalized from a free kick. Then, in the last minute, Stanley Matthews once again got the ball on the right wing.

What did he do? His favourite trick, of course! It worked as well as ever. Shooting past his full-back, Stanley raced to the by-line and pulled the ball back for his team-mate Bill Perry to whack into the goal. Blackpool 4, Bolton 3 – and Stanley Matthews had won his F.A. Cup winner's medal!

For most players, that might have been enough. Not for Matthews. He was a fitness fanatic who always trained hard and looked after himself. He still felt great – so why should he give up? His record in the following years will probably never be equalled:

- He played on for England for another three years, winning his last cap in 1957 at the age of 42.
- Four years on from that, in 1961 and at the age of 46, he left Blackpool. To retire? Not likely! He went back to Second Division Stoke City, the club he'd first played for as a 17-year-old.
- In 1963, at the age of 48, Matthews won another medal as Stoke won promotion to the First Division. Their average crowd had rocketed since his arrival … from 9,250 to over 25,000, and Stanley Matthews was voted Footballer of the Year for a second time.
- Two years later, the Stoke City team sheet still had his name on it. This time, there was a difference. It was able to say:

Right Wing: Sir Stanley Matthews

Yes, the Wizard of the Dribble had become the first footballer to be knighted while he was still playing.

But, retirement was near. There was just time for one more record. On 6 February, 1965, Stanley Matthews played his last game for Stoke. He was 50 years and 5 days old.

So, now you know what it takes to be a top footballer, who do you want to play for? There are some pretty famous teams around to choose from. How about St. Domingo's Park? Dial Square? Or there's the biggest of the lot, Lancashire and Yorkshire Railway Company Newton Heath. Who, who and who? Read on!

FOUL FOOTBALL CLUBS

Foul origins

The famous football clubs we know today started out in many different ways. For instance, the sound of church bells inspired quite a few teams to start up. Whether they called themselves foot-bellers and had teams with lots of wingers who played like angels isn't known!

- Everton began as St Domingo's F.C.
- Aston Villa was formed by members of the Villa Cross Wesleyan Chapel.
- Fulham started out as Fulham St. Andrews, after the name of their church.
- Swindon Town was formed by a keen football-playing vicar.

- Bolton Wanderers were originally Christ Church F.C.
- Celtic were formed by a priest, with the aim of raising money to feed the poor in East Glasgow.

Foul factory football

The other place in which men gathered in the mid-1880s was the factory in which they worked. As football grew in popularity, a number of these formed works football teams – some of which went on to become teams we know today.

Arsenal, for instance, was formed by workers at the Royal Arsenal Munitions Factory in Woolwich, London. (The workers made guns – which is why the club's nickname is "The Gunners".) They played their first games on a pitch behind the workshops under the name "Dial Square F.C."!

Can you pair these factories with the famous teams they produced?

1. George Salter Springs Works   a) Millwall
2. Singers Cycles   b) Stoke City
3. Thames Ironworks   c) Coventry City
4. Mortons Jam Factory   d) Manchester Utd
5. Staffordshire Railway   e) West Ham
6. Lancashire and Yorkshire Company Newton Heath   f) West Bromwich Albion

Answers:
1-f; 2-c; 3-e; 4-a; 5-b; 6-d

What shall we do in the winter?

Sometimes, a football club was only formed to provide something for a cricket team to do in the winter!

- Sheffield Wednesday were formed in 1867 by the members of the Wednesday Cricket Club.
- Tottenham Hotspur (1882) were formed by the Hotspur Cricket Club.

The foul landlord's team!

Finally, one famous team started out as the result of a foul! St Domingo's Park, now known as Everton, played at a ground in Liverpool. This ground was owned by an Everton supporter named John Houlding. The club paid their landlord £100 a year (probably letting him watch games for free as well) and everybody was happy.

Then Houlding put the rent up – to a whacking great £250 per year.

The conversation after that was short and sharp:

And so, Everton moved to a ground called Goodison Park. As for John Houlding, he'd now got a ground but no football team! So he promptly formed one, called them Liverpool, and they played at Houlding's ground – Anfield – from then on. Things are set to change, though. In 2008 both Everton and Liverpool announced plans for new grounds. They may even share one! Now why didn't Houlding think of that?

Don't foul me, sir!

Finally, some teams were formed by friends who'd enjoyed playing football (and kicking each other) at school and wanted to carry on playing the game (and kicking each other) after they'd left.

- Blackburn Rovers were formed by the former pupils of Blackburn Grammar School.
- Leicester City, then called Leicester Fosse, were started by the old boys of Wiggleston School. (It's not difficult to see why they chose the name Leicester – who'd want to play for a team called The Wigglers!)

There's even a famous team that was started by teachers!

- Sunderland were formed by the members of the Sunderland and District Teachers Association.

Who knows, maybe if you make up a team from your school friends today you'll end up beating Manchester United at Wembley!

Fair ladies football team names

The only trouble with team names nowadays is that they're pretty boring – all those Uniteds and Towns and Rovers. The names of ladies' teams are much more interesting. See if you can put together both halves of these names:

1. Villa	**a)** Roses
2. Doncaster	**b)** Lionesses
3. Millwall	**c)** Belles
4. Maidstone	**d)** Aztecs
5. City	**e)** Tigresses

Answers:
1-d; 2-c; 3-b; 4-e; 5-a

Foul football kit

You've formed your team. Now, what are you going to wear? Some simple shirts, with just one colour – or something a bit snazzier with stripes or hoops? How about shorts and socks? Something matching the shirts, of course, with every player wearing the same. This didn't happen in the early days! It took some time for football kit as we know it to come about.

Your foul football kit timeline:

1872 Standard kit for a footballer was: "plus-four" trousers tucked into socks which stretch up to the knees, football jersey … and bobble-hat! Every player in a team wore the same colour shirt, but they could choose whatever they liked for the rest!

1873 Footballer Lord Arthur Kinnaird could always be recognized on the pitch. He wore long white trousers and a blue-and-white cricket cap.

1879 A team called Sheffield Zulus played all their games dressed up as Zulu warriors!

1895 The British Ladies played a North vs South match. The Manchester Guardian reported: "The ladies of the North wore red blouses with white yolks, full black knickerbockers fastened below the knee, black stockings, red beretta caps, brown leather boots and leg-pads." Not much different to Manchester United today!

1900 Racehorse owner Lord Rosebery persuaded Scotland to play against England in his racing colours – primrose and pink! The Scots were tickled pink as well ... they won 4-1.

1909 Until now, goalkeepers wore the same shirts as the rest of their team. Now they started to wear different coloured jerseys.

1910 Kit became uniform all over. The way a player could look different was by using a snazzy belt – elastic hadn't arrived yet, so he still needed one to hold his shorts up!

1911 Superstitious goal-keeper Dick Roose played his 24th game for Wales wearing the same jersey. He hadn't washed it since his

52

first international in 1900, believing it would bring him bad luck.

1928 Arsenal and Chelsea wore numbered shirts – the first time they'd been used.

1930 Herbert Chapman (Tottenham) wore yellow football boots.

1933 Numbered shirts were worn for the first time in an F.A. Cup Final. Everton's players were numbered from 1-11 and Manchester City's from 12-22!

1937 The England team wore numbers on their shirts for the first time, and in 1939 shirt numbers were officially introduced.

1960 Football kit started to be made from a brand new light-weight material called nylon. Until now, shirts were made of heavy cotton, shorts were long and baggy, and socks made out of wool.

1972 Leeds Utd had numbers on tags hanging from their sock tops.

1974 The first shirt sponsorship. England signed a deal with the "Admiral" company.

Clubs weren't allowed to do the same though.

1980-2 Shirt sponsorship finally allowed. Liverpool (with Japanese electronic company "Hitachi") lead the way – except when their games are on BBC TV! The Beeb, which doesn't show adverts, bans them until 1982.

1988 Replica strips started to be sold in the shops. Now you could play for your favourite team in the park!

1996 David Seaman played in goal for England wearing a red jersey with yellow, green and blue splodges, red shorts with yellow, green and blue markings, and yellow, red and green hooped socks. It made the Zulus of 1879 look dull!

2008 After regular changes, even referees are now in on the act. They wear coloured shirts with sponsors logos – and special pockets for red and yellow cards!

Foul shorts stories

Football shorts have seen many ups and downs over the years. Here are some of them!

Knaughty knickers

1904 The Football Association are worried about shorts coming up. A rule is introduced saying, "Footballer's knickers must cover the knee". It's not known what the ref had to do if they weren't – send them off? (The players, not the shorts!)

What a rip-off!

1921 Jim Bowie (Rangers) was playing against Partick Thistle in the Scottish F.A. Cup Final when his shorts got ripped. While he was off the field changing them, the player he was supposed to be marking scored the only goal of the game!

How many legs?

1960 Celtic become the first, and only, club to number their shorts instead of their shirts.

A bum rap!

1979 Full-back Sammy Nelson (Arsenal) was being barracked by the crowd after scoring an own goal. To show them just what he thought, he dropped his shorts. Arsenal suspended him for two weeks. More of a full-backside than a full-back!

Foul nicknames

York City lost that particular nickname when they sensibly changed their shirts to  something not quite so 'Y'-out! Then they returned to being known by the nickname they'd always had: "The Minstermen" (not Mr Men!), from the city's famous York minster church. Here are some foul football nicknames. Can you match them to their teams?

1. The Villans   a) Derby County
2. The Pirates   b) West Ham
3. The Rams   c) Aston Villa
4. The Tigers   d) Manchester United
5. The Red Devils   e) Bristol Rovers
6. The Hammers   f) Leicester City
7. The Foxes   g) Hull City

Answers:
1-c; 2-e; 3-a; 4-g; 5-d; 6-b; 7-f

Foul football grounds

Congratulations! You've been picked for your favourite team! Now, where are you playing? At a magnificent stadium, of course!

Can you imagine it? You pull on your kit in the warm changing rooms, trot up the players' tunnel – and hear the roar of the thousands of spectators who've come to watch the match. You play a fantastic game on the beautiful green pitch and then, when the game is over (or before the game is over if you've been sent off!), it's back to the changing rooms for a lovely hot bath.

Right? Well, nowadays perhaps. But it wasn't always the way. In the early years you'd have found things a bit different. Then there were some pretty foul football grounds...

Chronic changing rooms

- When Bradford City were formed in 1903, their players changed in a hut at one corner of the pitch! The visiting team were better off – they changed in a small room at a nearby hotel.
- Play against Grimsby Town, and you'd find yourself in one of the second-hand beach huts they used as changing rooms.
- And at Huddersfield, the players changed in an old tramcar – which was also used as a ticket office! As for lovely hot showers...
- When Arsenal first moved to Highbury in 1913, the ground wasn't finished. Players had to wash in bowls of cold water – and anybody unlucky enough to get injured was trundled from the pitch on a milk cart!

Pathetic pitches

The problem with many grounds was that they had previously been waste land. When football clubs took them over, they often only spent money on trying to make more room for spectators. The playing surface itself was often left exactly at it was – and that was often pretty foul!

- Blackburn's first pitch had a pond in the middle of it! For matches, this was boarded over and turfs placed on top.
- Northwich Victoria's ground had a stream running alongside it. This needed to be boarded over for matches as well, so that corners could be taken! Maybe this explains why the club were only members of the Football League from 1892-94 and then they sank out of sight!
- Port Vale's pitch was described in 1884 as having no grass on it at all.
- Newcastle's pitch at St James's Park sloped by nearly six metres from one goalmouth to the other.
- And as for Manchester United, in 1890 the football correspondent of the Blackpool Gazette reported that it was so often under water he'd heard that the club's officials had been taking lifeguard training!

- In 1884, a Scottish Cup tie between Arbroath and Rangers was replayed after Rangers protested that the Arbroath pitch was too short. It was, too – by 28 centimetres. Rangers, who'd lost the first game 3-4, won the replay 8-1.

Football grounds are nothing like as foul nowadays, of course. Or are they…

- In 1953 an F.A. Cup qualifying match between Runcorn and Witton was abandoned when Witton walked off after Runcorn had scored. Why? Because the ball hadn't gone between the posts. The Runcorn goal had a hole in the side netting and the ball had gone through that!
- The Reading pitch was covered in bald patches at the start of the 1985 season. Their groundsman had accidentally watered it – with weedkiller!

Did you know?
A traditional football match takes place every
Christmas Day on Goodwin Sands, in Kent.
Does one team manage to beach the other? Or are
they always tide?

Foul weather

Football is a game played even in foul weather. And according to one newspaper reporter in 1900, over Wolverhampton's

ground, Molineux, it was very foul indeed…

Sometimes, though, the weather can get just too bad to play at all. In 1947 the frozen winter caused the football season to be extended to June, and in the equally bad winter of 1963 virtually no football was played at all for the first six weeks of the year.

On another occasion, foul weather decided the league championship. In 1904, Everton were beating Woolwich Arsenal 3-1 when fog came down and the game had to be abandoned. When the match was replayed, Everton lost 1-2 … and ended the season losing the title to Newcastle by just one point.

Foul football question:
How did foul weather cause West Ham and Millwall to begin a match in one century and finish in the next?

Answer:
Their first game, on 23 December 1899
was abandoned after 70 minutes because of fog. They were ordered to play the remaining 20 minutes when they met in the return fixture – on 28 April 1900!

Terrible tragedies

It's not possible to mention football grounds without remembering that, as well as brilliant football matches, they've also been the scenes of some terrible tragedies.

> ### *1902*
> # IBROX PARK STADIUM DISASTER

The wooden terracing at Rangers' ground, Ibrox Park, collapsed. Twenty-five fans were killed and hundreds injured.

> ### *1946*
> # TRAGEDY AT BURNDEN PARK

Metal barriers snapped at Bolton Wanderers' ground, Burnden Park. Thirty-three people were crushed to death.

> ### *1971*
> # RANGERS AND CELTIC FANS KILLED

Another tragedy at Ibrox, this time when barriers gave way on a staircase leading out of the ground. Sixty-six Rangers and Celtic fans died.

1985
INFERNO AT BRADFORD CITY

A fire raged through an old wooden stand during Bradford City's final home game of the season. Fifty-six supporters died.

1985
RIOTING AT HEYSEL STADIUM

The second tragedy of that awful year. Rioting at the Heysel Stadium in Belgium before the European Cup Final between Liverpool and Juventus led to a wall collapsing. Thirty-nine people were killed.

1989
WORST FOOTBALL TRAGEDY EVER

Europe's worst football ground tragedy took place at Hillsborough, before the F.A. Cup semi-final between Liverpool and Nottingham Forest. Overcrowding at the Liverpool end led to fans at the front being crushed against the fence surrounding the pitch. Ninety-five died.

Wonder-foul Wembley

If you're a footballer the one ground you really want to get to is Wembley Stadium, with its famous arch. It was opened in 2007 and, as it's the national stadium, only the biggest matches will be played there.

Work began in 2000 after the old Wembley (known as the Empire Stadium) was closed. That stadium was built in a year, and opened in 1923. The new Wembley took seven years to arrive! It finally opened in 2007 and had cost – how much?

a) £798 million

b) £750,000

Answer:
a) £798 million. The original Wembley Stadium cost £750,000. But as that's worth over £30,000 million today, perhaps the new Wembley was a bargain!

Here are some fantastic facts about the new Wembley's amazing arch:

- it weighs 750 tonnes (equal to 10 jumbo jets)
- it's 7 metres in diameter (wide enough for a train to pass through!)
- it's 315 metres long (that's about 3 football pitches)
- it's 133 metres high (over one football pitch)
- it can be lit up in different colours (including 'football pitch green')
- when lit up, it can be seen 13 miles away (unless it's foggy)
- it's fitted with a warning beacon for low-flying aeroplanes (which can be seen even if it's foggy!)

THE TOPS FOR BOTTOMS AWARD...

Wembley Stadium – which has 2,618 toilets, more than any other ground. Very convenient!

Wembley hosts all kinds of football matches – including rugby, football and American football. You could play your next school match there if your teacher could afford the bill! More than that, it holds pop concerts and even a motor racing event! It can be changed into an athletic stadium, too. But football is its main sport. The football final for the 2012 Olympics will be held there – see *Flaming Olympics* for full details of what happens!

The new Wembley Stadium is great, but it's important to remember that the old Wembley was great, too. This is what it looked like:

It's all gone now, of course, but the memories remain. If you ever get to go to new Wembley, here are a couple of things to look out for:

• The Bobby Moore Statue

This is outside the stadium, and was unveiled in 2007. But was Bobby Moore?

  a) A footballer

  b) A sprinter

  c) A pop star

Answer:
a) And not just any old footballer. He was captain of the England team which won the World Cup at the old Wembley in 1966.

• White Horse Bridge

The walk from Wembley Central station to the stadium takes you over White Horse Bridge. This name commemorates a real police horse – named Billy – and something that happened before the first-ever game at the old Wembley in 1923. Horses can't write, of course. But if they could …

WEMBLEY CONSTABULARY
INCIDENT REPORT
Investigating Officer : George Scorey.
Supported by : Police Horse 'Billy'. (Distinguishing marks – coloured white).
Report author : 'Billy'.

As my rider is still recovering from the events of 28th April 1923, this is my tale (Ha-ha!) – straight from the horse's mouth as you might say!

On the day in question we were summoned to the Empire Stadium, Wembley. The first ever F.A. Cup Final to be held there was due to take place between Bolton Wanderers and West Ham United. Arriving at the ground, I saw a large number of people behaving like horses. That is, they were jumping over fences!

My rider told them to stop. 'Whoa!' he cried, and I said 'neigh, neigh!' as well. It was no use. This horse could have been an old nag all afternoon and they wouldn't have taken any notice. Into the ground they galloped, all 200,000 of them.

What a nocturnal-lady-horse! (Sorry, I forgot this report is for humans. I mean, what a nightmare!). The ground was only built to hold 125,000; where would the other 75,000 fit?

We soon found out the answer to that question. When we got inside there were people all over the pitch, and none of them were footballers. It was very clear that unless we could produce a stable situation there would be no match!

I went to the centre of the pitch, then started to walk around in larger and larger circles. It made me
P.T.O.

feel quite giddy-up, but it worked. Slowly I started to jockey people backwards. Finally, and although people were almost standing on the white lines marking the pitch, there was enough room for the match to begin. Our job was done.

Signed,

(Billy)

Don't ask me who won. We left before hoof-time!

Bolton beat West Ham 2-0, but it was the white horse known as Billy who became the real star of the first Cup Final. Unless you were the West Ham trainer, that is...

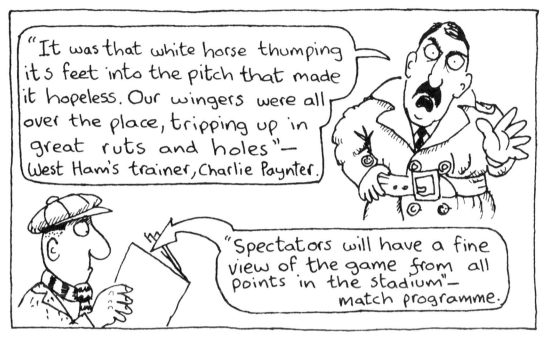

"It was that white horse thumping its feet into the pitch that made it hopeless. Our wingers were all over the place, tripping up in great ruts and holes" — West Ham's trainer, Charlie Paynter.

"Spectators will have a fine view of the game from all points in the stadium" — match programme.

Ready? It's time for the season to begin! You're going to be playing loads of games against different teams from all over the country.

What for? Good question! It's time to look at the trophies you'll be trying to win.

FOUL FOOTBALL COMPETITIONS

Nowadays there are pots of pots – usually called trophies – that football teams play for. But it wasn't always that way. Apart from playing other local sides in cup competitions most of the games played were friendlies against invited opponents. This didn't always work out…

Five foul excuses

Games were often cancelled at short notice, for all sorts of foul reasons. Which of these excuses were used?

1. The visitors arrived so late the crowd had gone home.

2. A star player wasn't available.

3. One of the teams didn't like the look of the pitch.

4. One of the teams had a more interesting game lined up.

5. It was raining.

If they think I'm going out in that, then they've got another thing coming!

Answer:
All of them – yes, even No. 5. To begin with, football was regarded as a 'fair-weather' game, and the teams would come off if it was raining!

The Football League

One man, William McGregor of Aston Villa, got in a foul temper because of all this messing about. His solution was to suggest to a number of other teams in the Midlands and the North that they should get together and play each other regularly in a league. That way, and by fixing dates for these matches, they'd know when and who they were playing for sure. What's more, so would the spectators!

In 1888, McGregor's idea came into being. The English Football League was formed, with just 12 teams.

Which of these teams were NOT in the 12?

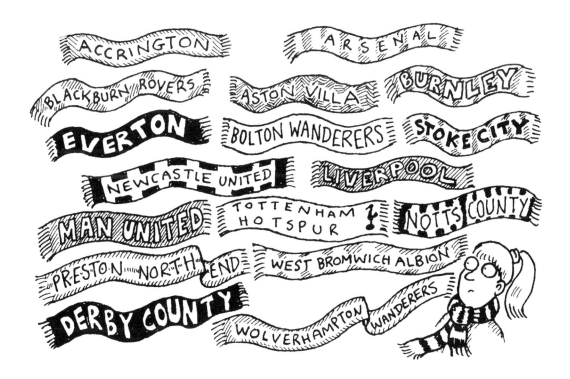

McGregor's idea was a great success. The Football League began to develop its own rules, and to grow and grow…

League timeline

1888 The league begins. Points are: 2 for a win, 0 for a draw or defeat. After just ten weeks, the rule changes to give 1 point for a draw.

1889 The first league champions are Preston North End. They don't lose a match all season and are nicknamed "The Invincibles".

1890 The Scottish and Irish Leagues are formed. In its first season, the Scottish League sees 409 goals scored in 90 matches – and there isn't a single 0-0 draw!

1892 The English league is extended to 16 clubs and a second league division is formed with a further 12 clubs. Promotion and relegation are invented as well.

Foul football question:
When did football teams play Test Matches?
Answer:
Between 1893 and 1898. To gain promotion, the Second Division sides not only had to finish in the top

three, they had to win a "test match" against one of the bottom three clubs as well, otherwise the First Division team kept their place. After 1898, two-up and two-down promotion and relegation became automatic – until playoffs bounced back again almost 90 years later, in 1987!

1892 Accrington resign from the league. They're the only club from the original 12 who've dropped out.

1893 Northwich Victoria finish with a miserly nine points and leave the league just two seasons after joining it. They never returned.

1895 To decide positions of teams who finish with the same number of points, "goal average" is introduced. It stays until 1975.

Foul football maths question:
Mudchester and Nutcastle finish in the top two with the same number of points. Mudchester scored 100 goals and let in 50, Nutcastle scored 50 and let in 24. Who wins the league on goal average?

Answer:
To work out a goal average, divide goals scored by goals let in. The team with the highest average is best. So Mudchester's average is exactly 2 which isn't as good as Nutcastle's average of 2 and a titchy bit. So, Nutcastle would have won the title, even though they'd almost certainly been a far more boring side.

1898 Second Division Darwen's goal average is pathetic. They finish bottom, having let in 109 goals in 17 away games and been beaten 10-0 three times – one of them by Loughborough, who came second from bottom! Surprise, surprise, Darwen were kicked out.

1903 Woolwich Arsenal join the Football League – the second team from the south of England to do so; Luton were the first, in 1897, but only lasted three years.

1919 Tottenham Hotspur are relegated – 5 years after finishing bottom of Division 1! The league was suspended during World War I and they dropped down to the Second Division when it restarted.

1920 By now, both the First and Second Divisions have expanded to 22 clubs each. The following season Southern League clubs form Division 3 (South).

1921 Division 3 (North) is formed, with 20 clubs. Southend finish bottom of Division 3 (South), scoring only 34 goals all season. Their top scorer is full-back Jimmy Evans, with 10 goals – all penalties!

1931 Arsenal are the first Southern club to win the League.

1938 Manchester City are the First Division's top scorers with 80 goals. Unfortunately, they'd let in 77 – so they ended up being relegated as well!

1950 Both of the Third Divisions expand to 24 clubs.

1958 Third and Fourth Divisions created. Clubs from the top halves of Division 3 (North) and Division 3 (South) go into Division 3, the rest into Division 4.

1960 Burnley become the First Division champions on the last day of the season – the only time during the season they have been in the top spot.

1961 Northampton win the Fourth Division and are promoted...

THE ROLLERCOASTER AWARD...

Northampton Town – who, between 1960 and 1970 go up or down six times! They started at the bottom (then called Division 4) in 1960/61, reached Division 1 by 1964/5 ... only to begin a slide which took them back to Division 4 by 1968/9!

1962 Accrington Stanley (not the same as 1892's  Accrington) resign from the Football League.

Fantastic football names quiz

When Stanley disappeared, the league lost one of its most entertaining team names. Here are ten other good 'uns who have disappeared over the years.

Which five were English and which five were Scottish?

1. Bootle (left in 1893), **2.** Lochgelly United (1926), **3.** Nithsdale Wanderers (1926), **4.** Nelson (1931), **5.** Glossop North End (1915), **6.** Stalybridge Celtic (1923), **7.** Vale of Leven (1926), **8.** Clackmanan (1926), **9.** Gainsborough Trinity (1912), **10.** Bathgate (1929)

Answers
English – 1, 4, 5, 6, 9; Scottish – 2, 3, 7, 8, 10.

1976 Goal difference replaces goal average as a way to encourage attacking teams.

1981 They still don't attack enough! A win is now worth three points.

1987 Play-offs are brought in to decide some promotion and relegation spots. Two years later, this was altered so relegation was automatic and play-offs were for promotion only.

1987 The bottom club in Division 4 can no longer beat the drop by applying to be re-elected. They're now automatically replaced by the champions of the Conference National League.

1989 Arsenal go to Liverpool for the last game of the season. If they win 2-0, they're champs; if they don't, Liverpool are champs. Arsenal win 2-0 … with their second goal coming from Michael Thomas in the last minute!

1992 The F.A. Premiership is established. All the First Division clubs resign from the Football League and transfer to the Premiership, leaving just the Second, Third and Fourth Divisions. Since having a Second Division as the top league sounds a bit daft, the Second Division becomes the Football League's First Division, the Third the Second and the Fourth the Third – get it? In other words, almost every club is promoted. The only ones who aren't are the relegated teams – they stay where they are!

2004 The teams in the Second and Third Divisions get promoted again! Their leagues are renamed Leagues One and Two. As for the First Division, that becomes … no, not the Zero Division: The League Championship.

2005/6 Chelsea win the Premier League for the first time. They're only the fourth club (after Manchester United, Arsenal and Blackburn) to win the title since the league was created.

2008 UEFA, the European Organising body, decide which is the top league in the whole of Europe. The winners – The Premier League!

2010 Barclays Bank's deal to sponsor the Premier League ends. Who will be next? How about: The Scholastic Children's Books 'Foul Football' Premier League!

The F.A. Cup

Although clubs spend the majority of their time playing league games, the Football Association Cup – or F.A. Cup as it is known throughout the game – is an older competition.

It was started in 1871, seventeen years before the Football League. In all, fifteen clubs took part – one of them, Queens Park, from Scotland – and was won by a team called the Wanderers. When you see how they did it, you might think they should have been called the Wonderers!

- Round 1 Their opponents, Harrow, drop out before the game is played.
- Round 2 They beat Clapham Rovers, 3-1.
- Round 3 They draw 0-0 with Crystal Palace (not the team we know today). There are no replays in the early rounds, so both teams go into the semi-final!
- Semi-Final They draw 0-0 with Queens Park, who then have to drop out because they can't afford the train fares to travel from Scotland to London for the replay. The Wanderers are in the Cup Final!
- Final Wanderers beat Royal Engineers 1-0, so with only their second victory in the competition, Wanderers become the first-ever holders of the F.A. Cup!

They went one better the year after, needing only one win to lift the F.A. Cup. How? Because, as holders, the rule then was that they went straight into the Final!

F.A. Cup timeline

1873 Wanderers play Oxford University in the second F.A. Cup Final. The match kicks off at 11 a.m., so that everybody can get away in time to watch the much more important Oxford v Cambridge Boat Race!

1874 Queens Park, unsuccessful in the F.A. Cup, win the first Scottish F.A. Cup Final.

1879 Rangers draw 1-1 with Vale of Leven in the Scottish F.A. Cup Final, having had a goal disallowed. Still miffed, they refuse to turn up for the replay and Vale of Leven are awarded the cup.

1885 Arbroath record the highest-ever Scottish F.A. Cup score when they beat Bon Accord 36-0 in a first round game. The Bon Accord

side played in their working clothes, without football boots, and with a midfielder in goal. The bored Arbroath keeper didn't touch the ball once.

1887 Preston knock up the highest-ever English F.A. Cup score, beating Hyde 26-0.

1901 Tottenham Hotspur become the only non-league side to win the F.A. Cup. They play in the Southern League.

1920 Shelbourne win the Irish Cup without having to play a final. The other semi-finalists are both disqualified – Glentoran for using a player they hadn't signed, and Belfast Celtic because somebody in their crowd opened fire with a gun!

1921 Birmingham City have the shortest-ever F.A. Cup run. They forget to send in their entry form!

1927 Welsh club Cardiff City become the only club to take the F.A. Cup out of England.

1930 Arsenal meet Huddersfield in the Final – and the teams come out side by side for the first time.

1946 Rochdale win their first F.A. Cup match since 1928, 18 years previously!

1950 Arsenal win the Cup without leaving London! They get four home draws, play their semi-final against Chelsea at Tottenham Hotspur's ground, and then go to Wembley for their 2-0 win in the Final against Liverpool.

1958 For the third season running, Leeds are drawn against Cardiff. And, for the third season running, Cardiff beat them 2-1.

THE SEVEN-GOAL LOSER AWARD...

Denis Law (Manchester City). In 1962, Manchester City played Luton in the FA Cup 4th round. City were winning 6-2, with all their goals scored by Law, when the match was abandoned due to a waterlogged pitch. When the game was replayed Law scored yet another goal – but Luton won 3-1!

1971 Ted McDougall scores nine goals for Bournemouth in their 11-0 win against Margate.

So, Dave, why are Wimbledon called The Crazy Gang?

1988 Dave Beasant of Wimbledon becomes the first goalkeeper to save a penalty in the F.A. Cup Final, as his team beats Liverpool 1-0.

1992 Liverpool v Sunderland. For the first time the losing team, Sunderland, go up to receive their medals first with Liverpool coming up second to get the Cup. But get a bit mixed up – and Sunderland get the winner's medals! The two teams have to swap them later.

2001-06 With Wembley Stadium being rebuilt, the FA Cup Final moves out of the country! For 6 years, it's played at the Millennium Stadium in Cardiff.

2008 With the game now back at the new Wembley, Cardiff reach the final! (But lose to Portsmouth).

Foul football trophy facts

1. The original F.A. Cup was bought for £20 and was 46cm high. It was stolen from a shop window in 1896 and melted down to make fake silver coins.

2. A second, identical, cup was made. It was used until 1911, when it was presented to Lord Kinnaird to mark his 21 years as F.A. President.

3. The present F.A. Cup was made in 1911. It is 48cm high, weighs almost 5kg, and was made in Bradford. (Bradford City won it that year, the only year they've ever been further than the sixth round.)

4. By 1992 the old trophy was too fragile to be chucked about by winning teams. An identical copy was made and is still in use.

The Football League Cup

Unlike the F.A. Cup, which can be entered by any club which is a member of the Football Association (and well over six hundred of them do enter it!) the League Cup can only be entered by the 92 members of the Premiership and the Football League.

It was started in 1960/61 and, in that season, not every member wanted to take part in it. Some thought there were already too many games being played.

Foul football odd-men-out

Five of these clubs didn't take part in the first League Cup; the other two met each other in the final. Which were they?

Answer:
Aston Villa beat Rotherham in the second-leg final; they lost the first leg 0-2, but won the second leg 3-0 to win 3-2 on aggregate.

For the first six years, the final of the League Cup was played over two legs. Only in 1967 did it move to a single match final, taking place at Wembley.

The Name Game

When it comes to names, the Football League Cup has undergone almost as many changes as the England strip ...

- In 1982, it became the first sponsored trophy. The sponsors were The Dairy Council, and the trophy became known as The Milk Cup! (Maybe it should have been called the Milk Bottle?).

- It kept this name until the end of the 1985/6 season. Then, from 1987/90 it was sponsored by the football pools company, Littlewoods, and became known as The Littlewoods Cup.
- From 1991/92 it changed again, becoming The Rumbelows Cup after the electronics company which sponsored it. Between 1993 and 2003 it was sponsored by Coca-Cola, then Worthington. Now (for a while) it's the Carling Cup.

THE MOST INSULTING NAME AWARD...

The Mickey-Mouse Cup – which was the name given to the League Cup by the clubs who didn't enter it when the competition first started.

Four trophies you've never heard of

Competitions come and go. Here are some that have definitely gone!

The FA Amateur Cup

Nowadays footballers are footballers. This certainly wasn't always the case. When the F.A. formed, footballers were either amateur (they didn't get paid for playing) – or professional (they did!). Entry to the Amateur Cup was limited to the amateur teams. It disappeared in 1974.

Did you know?

Being an amateur didn't stop you getting a big head. In 1895 the Old Carthusians were so confident of beating Middlesborough and retaining the cup they'd won the year before that they didn't bother to take it with them. They lost – and the trophy had to be delivered to Middlesborough some time later!

The Coronation Cup

This was played for just once, in 1953, to celebrate the Coronation of Queen Elizabeth II. Eight teams took part, four from England – Arsenal, Manchester United, Tottenham Hotspur and Newcastle United – and four from Scotland – Celtic, Aberdeen, Hibernian and Rangers.

Who won? Celtic, beating Hibernian 2-0 in the final.

The Ford Sporting League

This was a trophy for footballers who weren't foul. Points were given for good behaviour, and for goals scored.

Who won it? Oldham Athletic … and they've been the 'oldhers ever since! The competition lasted just one season, 1970/71.

The Watney Cup

This was a pre-season cup sponsored by the brewers Watneys and was played for by the two highest-scoring teams in each of the four divisions (excluding those who'd qualified for European competitions). Its first winners were Fourth Division team Colchester United, who beat First Division West Bromwich Albion 4-3 on penalties after drawing 4-4! The competition lasted four years, 1970–1973, and was the first trophy ever to use the penalty shoot-out as a decider.

It's been a brilliant season! Your team's won every trophy going, and you've played like a genius!

Now what?

Well, how's your German? How about your French, then? What about your Croatian? Dear me, you'd better start brushing up on your foreign languages. Your team's qualified for Europe and you've been picked for your country!

We're off to play some foul foreign football!

FOUL FOREIGN FOOTBALL

Having invented the game, England believed themselves to be the only country, apart from Scotland, Wales and Ireland, who could play a decent game of football – and they weren't so sure about Scotland, Wales and Ireland.

For a long time, they were right…

International games

- 1870 A game takes place between Englishmen and Scotsmen, in London. It's hardly a real international because both sides are picked by the English F.A., many of the Scots being selected for no better reason than that they've got Scottish-sounding names!

- 1872 sees the first real international between England and Scotland. In front of a crowd of 4,000 the two teams play out a 0-0 draw. Was it worth the effort?
- 1883 The Home International Championship begins. In this, the four "home" countries of England, (Northern) Ireland, Scotland and Wales play each other in a mini league competition. Scotland are the first winners.
- 1886 International "caps" are introduced – and used! Remember, this was when players really did wear caps on the pitch.

- 1890 Cocky England play two of their Home Internationals on the same day, fielding two different teams. One beats Wales 3-1 in Wrexham, the other whacks Ireland 9-1 in Belfast.
- 1908 A team of England amateur players win the football gold medal at the Olympic Games in London.
- 1912 England retain the Olympic gold medal in Stockholm. It's the last time they get anywhere near it.

Foul football question:
Where did an unofficial international between England and Germany take place in 1916?

Answer:
On a First World War battlefield. The East Surrey Regiment advanced on the Germans "kicking footballs before them".

And then it all started to go downhill...

- 1929 Almost 50 years after playing their first international, England taste defeat. They lose 4-3 away to Spain. The newspapers blame the heat, saying "beads of perspiration were dropping off the chins of our players as they ran about"!
- 1950 Disaster! In their first appearance in the World Cup competition, England lose 0-1 to the United States of America.
- 1953 The most famous pair of international thumpings in the history of the game. England lose 3-6 to Hungary at Wembley, their first home defeat at the hands of a team from outside the British Isles. Could things get any worse? Definitely. When they travel to Budapest

for the return game six months later, they lose 1-7.

- 1966 On top of the world again. England win the World Cup at Wembley.
- 1967 Scotland beat England 3-2 at Wembley, England's first defeat since winning the World Cup. The delerious Scottish fans take home bits of the turf as souvenirs.
- 1970 Disaster! Looking good in Mexico, England reach the quarter-finals of the World Cup and are 2-0 ahead against West Germany. Then the Germans score to make it 2-1 … they score again to make it 2-2 … and in extra time they score the winner.
- 1974 England, Wales and Ireland don't even qualify for the World Cup finals. Scotland do, but can't get past the first round.
- 1984 England and Scotland decide that Ireland and Wales aren't good enough, so they don't want to play the Home International Championship any more. The result of the last ever competition? First Ireland, second Wales!

- 1990 England and Scotland stop playing each other. From now on, the Home countries are like foreigners. The only time they'll play each other is when they're drawn together in either the European Championships or the World Cup…

The World Cup

The World Cup competition had been going for twenty years before England decided to join in the fun. It had first been played for in 1930 and was organized by FIFA – the International Federation of Football Associations.

On the face of it, the decision was a good one. The early World Cups were quite foul affairs…

The World Cup timeline

1930 The tournament was played in Uruguay, and the host country reached the final, where they played their deadly enemy Argentina. Just to make sure that it wasn't too deadly, the teams were guarded by soldiers with fixed bayonets and, before the final itself, spectators were searched for guns!

1934 The finals were played in Italy, and again the host country were the winners. It wasn't plain sailing though. Their drawn game against Spain was so dirty that 11 out of the 22 players weren't fit for the replay next day!

1938 In France, Italy retained their title. Again there was some foul stuff going on. When Brazil played Czechoslovakia, both sides ended up with nine players each. Two Brazilians and one Czech were sent off, and a Czech was carried off with a broken leg. It would have been 9-8 to Brazil, if the Czech goalkeeper hadn't played on with a broken arm!

Finally, England joined the rest of the world for the 1950 tournament in Brazil. The Home International Championship was used as the decider and, as winners, England qualified. As runners-up, Scotland could have gone too but preferred to stay at home. England soon wished they'd done the same. In a catastrophic match, they lost 0-1 to the USA and failed to qualify from their group.

In 1954, in Switzerland, they did a bit better and reached the quarter-finals before losing to Uruguay.

1958 was a special year. Each of the four home countries qualified for the Finals in Sweden, with Wales and Northern Ireland reaching the quarter-finals.

England were the only qualifiers for Chile in 1962, and got nowhere. Then came 1966...

90

The 1966 story

Everybody knows the story of the World Cup of 1966 – especially the Scots, the Irish and the Welsh who are always being told about it by the foul English!

After a dodgy start, England won through to the final at Wembley where they beat West Germany 4-2 after extra time. The match was full of drama. England came back from 0-1 down to go into a 2-1 lead with goals from Geoff Hurst and Martin Peters – only for Germany to equalize with almost the last kick of normal time.

Then, in extra time, England scored a disputed third goal. Hurst whacked the ball against the German crossbar and it bounced down. The referee, after talking to his linesman, decided that it had crossed the line, and the goal counted. Then, in the final minute, Hurst ran through to score England's fourth goal, and become the first player ever to score a hat-trick in a World Cup final.

But you knew all that, didn't you? So here's some foul 1966 facts that maybe you don't know...

- Before the tournament started, the trophy itself was stolen from an exhibition in London. It was found in a front garden – by a dog named "Pickles".

- The match ball was stolen too! As scorer of a hat-trick, Geoff Hurst would have expected to keep it as a souvenir. Instead the German player Helmut Haller, who'd scored his country's first goal, stuffed it up his shirt and took it home to Germany

- Geoff Hurst wasn't picked for the first three of England's games. He came into the team for the quarter-final against Argentina, scored the only goal, and stayed in the side.
- That match was held up for ten minutes. Argentina's captain, Antonia Rattin, was sent off for arguing with the referee and wouldn't go.

- When Bobby Moore, England's captain, went up to receive the World Cup from the Queen, he realised his hands were muddy. So he wiped them on the velvet covering the shelf in front of her!

Since then, things have been fairly foul...

Year	England	N. Ireland	Scotland	Wales
1970	qtr-finals	out	out	out
1974	out	out	1st round	out
1978	out	out	1st round	out
1982	qtr-finals	qtr-finals	1st round	out
1986	qtr-finals	1st round	1st round	out
1990	semi-finals	out	1st round	out
1994	out	out	out	out
1998	2nd round	out	1st round	out
2002	qtr-finals	out	out	out
2006	qtr-finals	out	out	out

Foul foreign club competitions

For a club side nowadays, doing well in one of the major domestic competitions means that the team qualifies to play in one of the big European competitions.

- From 2009-10 the top three Premier League teams play in the European Champions' League. The fourth-placed team go into a qualifying round; if they win, they play in the League as well. (So why don't they call it The European Champions' and Non-Champions' League? Don't ask!)
- The 5th-placed team in the Premier League qualify for the UEFA Cup. So do the FA Cup and League Cup winners (unless they're in the Champions' League in which case the FA Cup runners-up and the 6th-placed team get the places).

Playing in Europe is accepted as a good thing. But when it was first suggested that British teams should enter European competitions, some people cried "foul"...

- **1955/6** Chelsea win the League and qualify for the European Champions' Cup. The Football League advise them not to enter, saying they'll have trouble playing the extra matches. So Chelsea withdraw, leaving Scottish League team, Hibernian, to become the first British team in Europe. They reach the semi-finals!
- 1956/7 Manchester United are given the same advice by

the Football League. They ignore it, enter, beat Belgian side Anderlecht 10-0 in their first home game and also go on to reach the semi-finals!

From then on, British clubs played every year in Europe. Their record has been a mixture of fantastic, awful – and a period when the rest of the countries cried "foul!"

Tottenham Hotspur were the first British side to win a European trophy, the 1963 Cup Winner's Cup (a competition scrapped in 1999). In 1967, Scottish champions Celtic lifted the European Champions' Cup followed by Manchester United in 1968. At this time British clubs were fantastically successful. Between 1965 and 1984, they lifted the European and UEFA Cup nine times apiece, and the Cup Winner's Cup five times!

Banned

Then came the Heysel Stadium tragedy (see page 62). Liverpool supporters were found guilty of causing the disaster and, as part of the punishment, all British clubs were banned from European competitions until the start of the 1990-91 season.

Back with a bang!

The first season back it was again Manchester United who led the way, beating Barcelona in the 1991 Cup Winner's Cup final. Arsenal repeated the trick in 1994 and in 1999 Manchester United were the Champions' League winners with an amazing two-goals-in-extra-time victory against German team Bayern Munich! (United weren't the reigning Premiership champions, either. They'd qualified as League runners-up. Ah, well...)

Good News and Bad News

Between 2005 and 2008, English clubs appeared in the final every year. Some years it was good news and some years it was bad …

2005: Bad, then Good! At half-time, Liverpool were 0-3 down to AC Milan. But a fantastic second-half display saw them draw level at 3-3, then win the cup on a penalty shoot-out.

2006: Good, then Bad Arsenal were beating Barcelona 1-0. But with their goalkeeper Jens Lehman becoming the first player sent off in a European Cup Final, they ended up being beaten 1-2 .

2007: Bad AC Milan got their revenge for 2005, beating Liverpool 2-1.

2008: Good AND Bad, depending on who you support. In an all-English final, Manchester United beat Chelsea in a penalty shoot-out after the game had ended 1-1. For Chelsea's captain John Terry, it was very, very bad. Needing to score his penalty to win the match he slipped and hit it wide.

John Terry ended that game in tears, but the thought of retiring didn't enter his head. He knew that a footballer's career doesn't last very long. Most players have reached the end by the time they're 35. (This probably seems ancient to you, but it's not really. In most other jobs you can keep going until you're 65.)

So, it's time to think ahead. What are you going to do when you finish playing? Go and get another job, or stay in football somehow?

Many foul footballers do just that. How? By becoming foul managers, that's how! Read on for the lowdown on just how foul some of them have been!

FOUL FOOTBALL MANAGERS

Managers have a tough job. Think of all the things they've got to do – organize the players and decide what tactics to use, make the players believe they're absolutely brilliant even when they're totally useless, decide how much they're worth paying and try to give them less, decide how much they should be sold for and try to fool another manager into paying more – making sure they're not fooled in the same way when they buy one of the other manager's players. It's a foul job all right…

Managers who didn't manage for long:

- Bill Lambton was manager of Scunthorpe United in 1959. He lasted 3 days – the shortest managerial reign on record.
- In 1968, Tommy Docherty managed three clubs in six weeks: November – resigns as Rotherham manager; for 29 days, manager of Queens Park Rangers before resigning; December – manager of Aston Villa.
- In 1974, Brian Clough lasted 44 days at Leeds United.

Managers who found they couldn't manage:

- Alex Mackie was manager of Sunderland, then of Middlesborough. At both clubs he was found guilty of making illegal payments to players and suspended. He gave it all up and went off to run a pub.
- Syd King was West Ham's first manager, from 1901-1932. He did well, taking the club to the first Wembley F.A. Cup Final in 1923. But when the team was relegated in 1932 he started drinking. He was sacked after being rude to the directors and committed suicide a month later.

Foul formations

You're in the job. Now, how are your team going to play? In the early days of football, that wouldn't have been a problem. This would have been your line-up:

Yes, English football in 1880 was played with three defenders and seven attackers! When a forward got the ball he didn't pass it, but just dribbled with it until he lost it. (A bit like games in the playground). Great fun if you were the one with the ball, but pretty boring if you weren't! It was the Scottish teams who played football as a passing game. The English only started playing that way when the Scots came along and wiped the floor with them!

Gradually, though, formations changed. The forwards became fewer and the defenders greater, until this "classic" 1-2-3-5 formation developed, lasting up until the early 1960s:

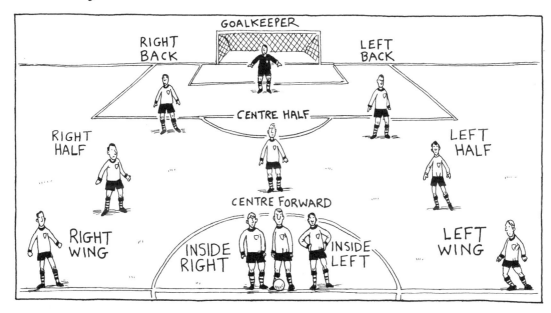

Formations since then have become bewilderingly different. Brazil led the world into 1-4-2-4 formations when they won the World Cup in 1958.

Then England played a 1-4-3-3 formation when they won the World Cup in 1966. Why? Because the manager, Alf Ramsey, decided he didn't have any decent wingers and told his full-backs to play there as well as in their own positions.

That's what managers have to do – make it up as they go along!

Fair tactics – or foul?

Managers have to come up with tactics to suit their team, and the match they're playing. Sometimes the tactics are fair – and sometimes they're foul!

Try this quiz to find out who did what!

1. Bob Paisley (Liverpool, 1974-83) would signal one of his players to go down after the next tackle. He'd then run on to the pitch to check how his player was. FAIR or FOUL?

2. Frank Buckley (Wolverhampton Wanderers, 1930s) thought his team played better in heavy conditions – so before every home game, he flooded the pitch! FAIR or FOUL?

3. In 1996, with Manchester United 12 points behind Newcastle in the league title race, United manager Alec Ferguson suggested that teams were trying harder against his team than against Newcastle. FAIR or FOUL?

4. Instead of talking to his players before the start of extra time in the 1991 F.A. Cup Final against Tottenham Hotspur, Notts Forest manager Brian Clough chatted to a policeman instead. FAIR or FOUL?

5. When Jose Mourinho took over as Chelsea manager

in 2004 he said: 'I am a special one' – suggesting that it would be the players' fault if they lost, not his! FAIR or FOUL?

6. Bob Paisley again. Once, when Liverpool were playing an F.A. Cup tie, a dog rushed on to the pitch. Paisley chased after it. FAIR or FOUL?

Answers:

1. FOUL. At the same time he'd be telling the ref how many bad decisions he'd made against his team, with the hope that the poor old ref would try to make up for it.

2. FAIR – at least it was at the time. Not long after, pitch flooding was banned.

3. FOUL – at least that's what Newcastle manager Kevin Keegan thought, ranting on radio that he'd love it if his team beat United. But they didn't. United won the league by 4 points.

4. FOUL. Notts Forest lost 2-1 after extra time.

5. FAIR – at the end of the season, Chelsea were champs!

6. FOUL and FAIR. Not actually caring if the dog fouled the pitch, Paisley gave his players instructions as he ran past them!

101

Foul training methods

Brian Clough was an interesting manager in many ways. His players would run through anything for him … as they proved one day. Out on a training run, Clough suddenly called for them to remove their tracksuit bottoms, carry a partner on their backs, and run through a clump of stinging nettles!

If anything, Clough was simply returning to the old ways. In the early days of football, using a ball in training was thought to be a foul way of doing things. The players simply ran around and did exercises to keep fit. The idea was that, by not seeing a football all week, when Saturday came around they'd want it all the time!

This didn't apply to Chelsea, though. In the 1960s and 1970s two of their players, Peter Osgood and Alan Hudson, formed a "Monday Club" for training. Every Monday, they refused to do any training at all!

Terry Venables had the idea of putting his players under the influence. When he was manager of Crystal Palace in 1979, he called in a hypnotist to work with the players. At the end of the season, Palace were promoted!

Malcolm Allison, Manchester City manager, thought the players should hypnotise themselves. He gave each player a photocopied sheet:

Allison lasted two years, from 1971-73. That's the problem with being a manager. Sooner or later, you won't.

More than anything, though, a manager has to give his team confidence that they can win. Nobody was better at this than Bill Shankley of Liverpool (1959–74). He'd turn up in the changing room and say to his team: "I've just seen the other lot come in, boys. They look like they've been out all night. They're frightened to death!"

Foul managers' rules

As manager, you can't stand any messing about. Your players have got to toe the line, not kick up trouble. So, what do you do? You lay down some club rules. Here's a rule quiz. Which of these have been club rules at some time?

10 FOUL MANAGERS COMMANDMENTS

1) THOU SHALT NOT GO BOOZING BEFORE THE GAME

2) THOU SHALT NOT SMOKE

3) THOU SHALT NOT DRINK TEA ON TRAIN JOURNEYS

4) THOU SHALT NOT RIDE A MOTORBIKE

5) THOU SHALT NOT PASS THE BALL SIDEWAYS

6) THOU SHALT NOT BLOW OFF IN THE CHANGING ROOM!

7) THOU SHALT NOT LIVE MORE THAN 40 MILES FROM THE TOWN HALL

8) THOU SHALT NOT LEAVE YOUR FOOTBALL SHIRT INSIDE OUT

9) THOU SHALT NOT COMMIT A FOUL FOUL

10) THOU SHALT HAVE A BATH EVERY THURSDAY

Answers:

All of them have been rules for one club or another!

1, 2 – most clubs; 3 – Manchester City; 4 – Bolton; 5 – Notts Forest (by Brian Clough on his defender, Kenny Burns, who he wanted to pass forward more!); 6 – Bury (a rule that caused a bit of a stink!); 7 – Middlesborough; 8 – Non-league side Peterlee Gamecock FC; 9 – Arsenal (In 1933! After Tommy Black, the Arsenal left-back, committed a bad foul in the F.A. Cup tie that Arsenal sensationally lost to Walsall, manager Herbert Chapman said:"What you did was disgraceful; you will never wear an Arsenal shirt again." He didn't); 10 – Leeds United. (As a way of encouraging team togetherness, manager Don Revie (1961-74) insisted on the players having a bath every Thursday – together! Hopefully he insisted on rule 6, too!

Foul transfers

One of the manager's jobs is to buy and sell his players. He tries to sell the useless ones for as much as he can – and buy players who are good (he hopes) as cheaply as he can.

That's got harder and harder over the years.

Your transfer spiral timeline.

1899 The Football Association suggest maximum transfer fee of ... £10

1902 Alf Common, Sheffield Utd. to Sunderland, £500

1905 Alf Common, Sunderland to Middlesborough, £1,000

1925 David Jack, Bolton to Arsenal, £11,000

1961 Denis Law, Manchester City to Torino, £100,000

1977 Kevin Keegan, Liverpool to Hamburg (Germany), £500,000

1979 Trevor Francis, Birmingham to Notts Forest, £1,000,000

1981 Bryan Robson, West Bromwich to Manchester Utd., £1,500,000

1987 Ian Rush, Liverpool to Juventus, £3,200,000

1991 David Platt, Aston Villa to Bari, £5,500,000

1995 Andy Cole, Newcastle to Manchester Utd., £7,000,000

1995 Stan Collymore, Notts Forest to Liverpool, £8,500,000

1996 Alan Shearer, Blackburn to Newcastle, £15,000,000

1999 Nicolas Anelka, Arsenal to Real Madrid, £22,500,000

2001 Juan Veron, Lazio to Manchester United, £28,100,000

2002 Rio Ferdinand, Leeds United to Manchester United, £29,100,000

2006 Andriy Shevchenko, AC Milan to Chelsea, £30,800,000

2008 Robinho, Real Madrid to Manchester City, £32,500,000

Here are some foul transfer tales:

- In 1919, Leeds City were expelled from the league. Their whole team was auctioned! Individual players fetched between £250 and £1,250 with the whole lot fetching a grand total of about £10,000! One of the £250 players was Bill Kirton. He was sold to Aston Villa – and scored the winning goal in the Cup Final!

- In 1925, Arsenal wanted to buy star forward Charlie Buchan from Sunderland...

That was the deal. Buchan promptly scored 21 goals that season, and Henry Norris (the Arsenal Chairman) had to fork out the £4,100!

THE KICKING BOTH WAYS AT ONCE AWARD...

James Oakes – who, in 1932/3 managed to play for both teams in the same match! He played for Port Vale v Charlton, but the game was abandoned before the end. When the replay came around, though, jumping James was playing against Port Vale; he'd been transferred to Charlton. Good decision – Charlton won!

- Jimmy Greaves should have been the first £100,000 player when Spurs bought him from AC Milan. Bill Nicholson, Spurs' manager, didn't want him to be stuck with that honour though, so he got the Italians to knock a pound off the fee!

- Andriy Shevchenko joined Chelsea from AC Milan in 2006 for £30 million. Two years later he was back at Milan after scoring just 9 goals for Chelsea – that's over £3 million per goal!

- Clive Allen was transferred from Queens Park Rangers to Arsenal in the summer of 1980 for £1,200,000. Before the season started, and before he'd played a game for them, Arsenal sold him to Crystal Palace for the same amount! Was Allen bothered? Not really – his share of each fee was £50,000!

- It doesn't always work out like that. Before it became legal to pay players a signing-on fee, different arrangements had to be made. When Jimmy O'Neill moved from Everton to Stoke, he had to move house as well. Stoke paid for a new cooker for his kitchen!

Moneybags!

Footballers earn plenty of money, don't they? Well, some of them do. Many of them don't. Money has always played its part in football, even when it wasn't supposed to. In the early days, every footballer was an amateur. In other words, they played the game for love, not money. Then organized competitions like the F.A. Cup came along. Teams wanted to win … in order to win they needed the best players … and the way to get the best players was to pay them!

This state of affairs – called professionalism – crept in slowly. In 1879, the little Lancashire side Darwen reached the last six of the F.A. Cup, holding the mighty Old Etonians to two drawn games before being beaten in the third. Their star players were two Scots, who'd been "persuaded" to join Darwen. Rumours grew that after each game pound notes would appear in their boots as if by magic. Were the rumours true? Nobody would admit it, but Darwen was an awfully long way to come from Scotland for a game of football…

Arguments raged on for a few years. In 1882, Preston North End were accused of using professionals in an F.A. Cup game. Much to everybody's amazement, Preston admitted it, saying, "Everybody else does, why not us?" Preston were thrown out of that season's F.A. Cup competition but within three years, the payment of players in England became legal.

In Scotland it took a little longer. Rangers, who regularly entered the F.A. Cup, found themselves drawn against a professional side. They withdrew in protest, and were fined 50p by the F.A.!

Two years later, Scottish clubs were banned by their own F.A. from entering the English cup. The problem then, however, was that all the best Scottish players were racing over the border to play for English teams! The move was on for Scottish players to become paid. In 1890 the Scottish League was formed. It was now only a matter of time before professionals were accepted in Scotland.

"You might as well try to stop the flow of the Niagara with a kitchen chair as endeavour to stop the tide of professionalism."

J.H. MacLoughlin, who helped start the Scottish League.

In 1893, the Scottish F.A. gave in and professional players were accepted. So, how much did a professional footballer earn? When you find out you'll wonder what all the fuss was about...

Sometimes it wasn't as much as that! In 1902, after the Stockport County players hadn't been paid for weeks, the players revolted against their management. Picking their own team, they grabbed all the gate money and shared it out for their wages!

A footballer's pay was actually very foul for another 60 years. During that time, footballers couldn't be paid more than a maximum wage. For a while this was £8 per week, then £10, until by the 1950s it had risen to £20 per week (worth £500 today). And you couldn't earn more than this amount however good you were, or whatever team you played for. An international player in a championship-winning side could be earning exactly the same amount as a player at the bottom of the Fourth Division.

Why was this the rule? Because it was thought that by having every club paying its players the same wages, there'd be less danger of just a few rich clubs grabbing all the best players. The players didn't see it that way, though. In 1961, led by Jimmy Hill, the Chairman of the Professional Footballer's Association they threatened to go on strike!

Almost at once the Football League agreed to scrap the maximum wage rule – and from then on, players could be paid as much as their clubs wanted.

Was that a good thing? For the players, yes! In 2008, Frank Lampard of Chelsea was offered a new contract at £140,000 a week. He turned it down – because his captain, John Terry was earning £150,000 a week!

Foul frauds

Wherever there's money, there'll be those who want more. As football became more popular, so did betting based on the results of matches. "Odds" would be offered for predicting which team would win a match, or for predicting that it would be a draw, or even for saying what the exact score would be. So it was only a matter of time before some foul footballers got their heads (and feet) together and tried to "fix" matches.

- In 1915, big bets were taken that Manchester United would beat Liverpool 2-0 in their match at Easter – which they did! After an investigation, no less than eight players (four from each side) were found guilty of rigging the match and banned for 30 years. Apart from one, they were all allowed to play again after the end of the First World War in 1918.
- In 1965, ten foul footballers were found guilty of fixing matches and sent to prison. Two of them, Peter Swan and Tony Kay (both Sheffield Wednesday, 1960s) had played for England.

Butterfingers Bailey

One surprise result which wasn't as suspicious as it seemed took place in 1909. After a superb run of goalkeeping in which he only conceded three goals in five games, A. Bailey (Leicester Fosse) suddenly let in 12 goals in one game! He was accused of taking a bribe, and then the real reason came out. He'd been to a wedding a few days before the match, got drunk, and hadn't recovered by the time he went in goal. He was probably seeing two balls and didn't know which one to save!

The game's over. There's only one job left to do – say a few words for the TV cameras and the newspaper reporters…

Foul football managers' quotes

So, do you fancy being a manager after all that? No? Well, there is another job in football. There are good things about it, and there are bad things.

The good side is that it's a job that gets you right into the centre of the action. You'll get plenty of excitement, and for much of the time the crowd will be roaring for you!

The bad side of the job is that you can be sure the crowd will be roaring some pretty foul things.

Yes, you could be the man in the middle. The referee…

114

FOUL REFEREES

Who'd be a referee?

Some would say that being a referee is the foulest job going. Has it always been that way?

Your foul referee's timeline.

1873 The referee had a cushy job. All the hard work was done by two umpires, one supplied by each of the two teams. Each umpire looked after one half of the pitch. The referee's job was to stand on the touchline and make a final decision if the two umpires couldn't agree. Oh yes, the umpires didn't have to make a decision either, not unless one team appealed – like in cricket!

1878 He doesn't shout any more. Whistles are introduced.

1891 With disputes getting more and more common, the referee and umpires change places. The ref moves to the centre of

the pitch and umpires, now called linesmen, move to the touchlines. Each linesman has to run up and down the whole length of the pitch.

1894 Players no longer have to appeal cricket-style. The referee is given complete control over the game, making decisions whenever he sees something wrong. This doesn't stop the players appealing, of course!

Foul refereeing question:
In 1894, Sunderland beat Derby in the longest league game ever played, but they were not sure what the score was. How could this be?

Answer:
The game began with a linesman in charge because the referee was late. When he finally turned up at half-time, with Sunderland 3-0 ahead, he used his new-found power and insisted on the whole game being played from the start. Sunderland scored another 8, meaning that they played for 135 minutes and either won 8-0 or 11-0!

Did you know?
- During a match, the referee runs about seven miles.
- Referees have to retire at the age of 48.

- Premier League referees can earn about £60,000 per year. Not much when many of the players they're controlling earn the same amount every week, but a big improvement on early payments. When the football league began in 1888, the match referee got 52½p (worth £42 today).
- Every league referee has to undergo a regular fitness test…
- and an eyesight test!

Tell that to one ref…
- In a game between Everton and West Bromwich Albion, referee Keith Butcher gave a penalty to Everton when everybody in the ground knew it should have been a free-kick to West Bromwich. That's when he found out – he was colour-blind!

Foul play! Red card!

One of the more dramatic sights in a football match is that of the referee waving the red card. He's only been able to do this since 1976 of course, as before that they weren't in use. When a player was sent off then, the usual thing was for the referee to point to the player's tunnel, as long as he could remember where it was!

Foul footballers can be sent off for seven foul reasons:
1. Serious foul play
2. Violent conduct
3. Spitting
4. Stopping a goal chance by handball
5. Swearing or making rude signs
6. Stopping a goal chance by a foul
7. A second 'yellow'card' offence; that is, one offence FOULowing another!

117

There have been some other reasons, though...

Foul decisions

- **The team that sent themselves off.**
  In 1891, Burnley were beating Blackburn 3-0 when one man from each side was sent off for fighting. Blackburn didn't like the decision and the whole team walked off in protest!

- **The referee sent off by a player.**
  In 1930, Sheffield were playing Glasgow in their annual inter-City game. In those days, referees wore jackets but on this occasion the referee, a Mr Thompson, left his off and started the match in his shirtsleeves. The trouble was, he was wearing a white shirt – and Sheffield's colours were white shirts and black shorts. After a couple of minutes the Sheffield skipper, Jimmy Seed, asked the ref to go off and change, saying, "I keep passing to you!"

- **The referee who sent himself off because of the player who wouldn't be sent off.**
  When William Cook (Oldham, 1915) refused to leave the pitch after being sent off in a match against Middlesborough, the referee sent himself off, and abandoned the game. Cook was suspended for one

year for his crime, which wasn't much of a hardship because all league games were cancelled for the next five years because of the First World War.

- **The referee who didn't send anybody off.**
The 1913 F.A. Cup Final was the occasion for a running battle between two players, Harry Hampton (Aston Villa) and Charlie Thompson (Sunderland). Even though the foul pair frequently came to blows, Mr Adams, the referee, didn't send either of them off. Afterwards, though, both players were suspended by the F.A. for what went on – and so was the referee, for being too soft!

Did you know?

Fulham player Paul Went was a fluent speaker of Italian. Playing in a cup match, he swore at the referee in Italian, and got booked!
The match was in the Anglo-Italian Cup, and the referee knew the rude word because he spoke Italian too!

Six foul records

- Alec Dick (Everton, 1888) was the first player to be cautioned in a Football League game, for swearing at another player. Apart from booking him, the referee ordered Dick to apologise to the player he'd sworn at!

- The fastest sending off during play is that of Kevin Pressman (Sheffield Wednesday) on 13th August 2000. Playing in goal against Wolves, quick-fire Kevin lasted just 13 seconds before being sent off for handling the ball outside his penalty area.

- The fastest sending-off for a substitute can't be beaten – because it's 0 seconds! Coming on for Swansea in 2000, Walter Boyd elbowed an opposing player and the referee sent him straight back off again!

- Willie Johnstone (Celtic) was sent off 15 times between 1969 and 1983.

- Kevin Moran (Manchester Utd., 1985) was the first player to be sent off in an F.A. Cup Final. His team still managed to beat Everton 1-0. Moran wasn't allowed to go up and collect his medal, he had it given to him later.

- Colchester scored a foul double in 1993. Playing against Hereford, their goalkeeper was sent off for a professional foul. On came their substitute keeper – only to be sent off for a professional foul as well! Surprise, surprise, Colchester lost 0-5.

120

Referees get used to being shouted at from all quarters. But there's one insult, decided the Scottish F.A. in 1996, that simply cannot be tolerated…

A certain John Neilson, playing for a team called Easthouses Lily in the East of Scotland league, was sent off. What did Neilson then do? Shout at the referee? Bop him on the nose?

No. While the match was going on, Neilson crept to the referee's changing room, and cut his socks in half!

The Scottish F.A. banned him for two years.

Penalty, Ref!

The forward's on the move. Past one player he goes, then another. He's into the penalty area. A defender moves in to tackle – and down goes the forward!

"Penalty, Ref!"

Everybody's looking at you. What do you do? Shake your head and run off in the opposite direction, or blow your whistle and point to the penalty spot?

You point to the spot, and the roar from the crowd can be heard in the next town … unless you've given a penalty against the home team, of course, then you're wishing you were in the next town. Ah well, it's all part of the fun of being a referee.

Here's a ref's guide to penalty pandemonium...

1891 The penalty law is brought in on 3 March. Three days later, the first-ever penalty is awarded at Airdrie, in a Scottish League game. It then has to be un-awarded when the referee remembers that the law isn't due to take effect until the following season!

1904 By now, refs are getting the hang of things. Four penalties are awarded in a match between St Mirren and Rangers – 3 to St Mirren and 1 to Rangers.

1913 The first-ever penalty is awarded in the F.A. Cup Final proper, to Aston Villa in their match against Sunderland. Villa's Charlie Wallace misses it! (But his team go on to win 1-0.)

1924 Crewe Alexandra play Bradford Park Avenue and four penalties are awarded in five minutes!

1945 The rules concerning penalties are quite clear: the goalkeeper mustn't move before the ball is kicked, neither must any other player enter the penalty area. In the Scottish League game between Kilmarnock and Partick Thistle, the referee obviously knew the rule off by heart. When Kilmarnock were awarded a penalty, he made them retake it seven times for various infringements. When, finally, a kick was taken that he was happy with, the Partick goalie saved it!

1980 The referees don't see things Liverpool's way. They went almost a year, and 53 matches, without getting one.

Penalty puzzler

The referee can't win. In an international match in 1996, Ecuador were awarded a penalty. This happened...

Matamba of Ecuador strides up...
... whacks the ball into the net...
but his boot comes off and flies into the net as well!
"Take it again," says the referee. This time...
Matamba of Ecuador strides up...
... but whacks the ball against the bar...
while his boot comes off again, this time hitting the post!
"No goal," says the referee.

Afterwards they check the rules – which fail to mention boots going into the goal, hitting the post or anything else. The ref was wrong, and the first goal should have been allowed.

124

The world's worst refereeing decision?

On 25 May 1964, Argentina played Peru in an Olympic Games qualifying tie. The match took place in Lima, the capital of Peru. Argentina were winning 1-0. Then, with just two minutes to go, Peru scored, only for the referee to disallow the goal.

This caused a riot to break out in the crowd. Police tried to stop it by using tear gas, but instead they started a panic. Three hundred and fifty spectators were killed and one thousand two hundred injured.

Afterwards the referee could only say, "Maybe it was a goal. Anyone can make a mistake."

So, maybe you don't fancy being a referee either. In that case, there's only one thing left … be a football supporter!

Trace your ticket! Root around for your rosette! Slip on your shirt! Scour around for your scarf! Rattle your rattle!

We're off to the match!

FOUL FANS

There's nothing wrong with being a plain old spectator, y'know. After all, it's the football fans who pay the entrance fees which help to pay the players and everybody else. Even if it isn't very much…

Foul football question:
How much did ladies have to pay to watch football matches in 1890?
Answer:
Nothing. They were let in free. The minimum charge for men was about 3p.

That doesn't sound a lot, but then you weren't getting a nice comfy seat in the grandstand either. For 3p, you ended up on a mound of earth behind the goal!

Yes, true football fans are prepared to put up with any conditions, however foul.

When non-league Yeovil played Sunderland in the fourth round of the F.A. Cup in 1949, they cashed in by adding stacks of extra seating. Fans who paid $37\frac{1}{2}$p to get in, found themselves sitting on beer crates!

True fans

A true fan is one who supports his or her team come what may, through thick or thin, promotion or relegation, ups and downs, ins or outs, no matter what it costs.

Maybe…

- **The true fan watches the match.** In 1902, Gainsborough were already bottom of Division Two when they faced Blackpool in an end-of-season match. When a fire broke out in a nearby building, most of the fans left the game and went to watch the fire. The true fans who stayed to watch saw one of their team's only wins that season!

- **The true fan always turns up.** And sometimes they wish they hadn't bothered! In 1921, not only were Stockport already relegated but they weren't allowed to use their own ground for their final match either. The match, against Leicester, was played at Old Trafford. Just 13 true fans turned up to watch – and were rewarded with a 0-0 draw.

● **The true fan stays to the end of the game.** With just five minutes of the 1979 F.A. Cup Final to go, thousands were leaving Wembley with Arsenal beating Manchester Utd. 2-0. They missed the most exciting finish in Cup history, with three goals being scored in three minutes as Manchester Utd. scored twice to draw level only for Arsenal to score again to win the match 3-2.

● **The true fan doesn't like being cheated.** "Ticket touts" try to make money by selling match tickets at more than their face value. In 1959, Third Division club Norwich City were having a brilliant run in the F.A. Cup and had been drawn at home to Tottenham

Hotspur in the fifth round. When some true, but ticketless, fans met a tout who was selling tickets at over 15 times what he'd paid for them, they paid him face value for his tickets – then chucked him in the River Wensum!

● **The true fan likes to see his team win – but fairly.**
In 1939, England were playing Italy, and the Italian Crown Prince was guest of honour. When Italy had a goal allowed, even though it was clearly handball, the Prince was so embarassed he wanted to go down to the pitch and tell the referee he'd got it wrong.

- **True fans chant for their favourite player.** In the 1970s, Coventry City used to have an advertisement which showed their team running out on to the pitch with the fans running out behind them. It had a caption saying, "This Saturday we're fielding 30,000 – make sure you're one of them." One of the true fans in this picture was a grandmother named Mrs Ridlington. Thereafter, whenever Coventry were playing badly, the crowd would start to shout, "Bring on Mrs Ridlington!"

- **True fans move about!** For the whole of the 1992 season, Arsenal kicked towards a North Bank packed with fans who didn't move and didn't make a sound! The ground was being rebuilt, and the fans weren't real – they'd been painted on a massive board behind the goal!

But what about when the football's at its worst, when your team is playing terribly, or the game is as boring as Maths on a Monday morning? Then, even the true fan can turn into a bit of a foul fan…

● In 1898, promotion from the Second to First Division was decided by "test matches" played out by the top two in the Second Division and the bottom two in the First Division. The problem was that they weren't played as knock-out games but as a mini-league competition. By the time Stoke and Burnley came to play their final game, both only needed a draw to be promoted. So, the two teams decided, a draw was what they would play for – and neither team even tried to score a goal. Finding they'd paid to watch the most boring game ever, the fans decided to make their own entertainment by pinching the ball whenever it was kicked into the crowd.

Final score: shots during the match 0, footballs stolen 5!

THE HAIR TODAY, NEARLY GONE TOMORROW AWARD...

George Best (Manchester United, 1966).
At the end of the 1966 Manchester United vs Benfica European Cup quarter-final in Lisbon, Portugal, a fan leapt over the fence surrounding the pitch and raced towards Best with a butchers' knife in his hand. It wasn't as bad as it sounds, though. The knife-wielder was really a true fan. Best was known as 'El Beatle' because of his long hair and the fan just wanted to cut himself a lock of it as a souvenir!

Fans in action!

Most fans can only dream of playing in a big match. For some of them, though, dreams have come true…

True fans are there when they're kneeded

A fan played a big part in the first Scottish F.A. Cup Final, between Queens Park and Clydesdale, when Clydesdale's forward James Long smacked the ball past the Queens Park goalie and into the net. At least it would have been into the net if they'd been invented, but this happened in 1874, all of 16 years before goal nets were introduced. So

what happened was that the ball shot between the posts, hit a spectator on the knee, and bounced out again. The referee disallowed the goal and Queens Park ended up 2-0 winners.

Booting for Bootle

In the 1880s Bootle were briefly the top team in Liverpool – bigger than Everton, and certainly bigger than Liverpool who weren't founded until 1892! And yet, just before a match in 1881, Bootle suddenly found themselves with only eight players. Not so good when the match was an F.A. Cup first round tie against Blackburn Law! So Bootle did the only thing they could, and asked three spectators to play for them.

Whoever the fans were, they must have been pretty good. Bootle won 2-1. Maybe they should have signed the fans on, too. When they played Turton in the next round with their full team, Bootle lost 0-4!

Collecting for Christmas

Brighton weren't so good at picking fans. On Christmas morning, 1940, they'd set out for a game against Norwich with only five players, hoping to collect a few more on the journey. (This sounds crazy, but it was fairly normal during the Second World War when players were stationed all over the country). Anyway, it didn't happen. By the time they reached Norwich they were still short, so they did a Bootle and recruited some soldiers from the crowd to make up their team … and lost 0-18!

Foul football hooligans

We're not going to devote any space at all to the foul types who go to football matches just to cause trouble. Football is a great game, and can do without them.

Foul football reporting

When real fans come home from the game, have they had enough? Of course not! What they then want to do is to read about the match in the newspapers or watch it again on the television.

The media have been reporting on football ever since the game began. And sometimes they've made a pretty foul job of it…

Naughty newspapers

When the Football League began in 1888, there were only two ways of finding out how your favourite team had got on: go to the match, or buy a newspaper. With no radio until 1927, and no regular television highlights until the mid 1960s, the newspapers had no rivals.

At first, that was just as well. Before 1900, photographic techniques weren't good enough for good pictures to be taken of football action. Photographs of running players came out all blurred, not because they were too fast, but because the cameras were too slow. So, instead of photographs, newspaper readers were given real pictures ... drawn by artists!

With the arrival of better photography, together with newspapers like the Daily Mirror which showed plenty of photographs, the Sports Page arrived. And with them came the headlines...

The 'WOW!'-Factor Quiz

Here are some lines and headlines taken from the sports pages over the years. Replace **WOW!** by one of the following: bores, disaster, ee-aye-addio, king, only, plastic, school, snatch, turnip, Wimbledon.

1. Although WOW! 63,102 people passed through the turnstiles...
Athletic News, 1903

2. Any one of our WOW! teams could easily have given the Paris team of yesterday a beating.
Daily Express, 1904

3. **The WOW! sees Burnley win the Cup.**
Daily Mirror, 1914

4. **Our biggest international WOW! for 46 years.**
Sporting Chronicle, 1928

5. **WOW!, the Reds have won the Cup!**
Liverpool Football Echo, 1965

6. **Sorry, lads – you're WOW!** *The People*, 1971

7. **The Big WOW!** *Daily Mirror*, 1978

8. **Fantastic on WOW!** *Daily Star*, 1981

9. **Game, Set and Match to WOW!**
Sunday Express, 1988

10. **Ta Ta WOW!** *The Sun*, 1993

Answers:
1. only – In 1903, that was thought of as a small crowd!
2. school – after Arsenal had beaten a visiting French team by 26 goals to 1!
3. King – after King George had become the first monarch to get a free ticket to the Cup Final.
4. disaster – after England lose 0-5 to Scotland.
5. Ee-aye-addio – echoing the Liverpool fan's song. Liverpool had beaten Leeds 2-1 to win the F.A. Cup for the first time ever.
6. bores. *The People* newspaper's verdict on Arsenal's style of play.

7. Snatch – after ITV had sneaked in and bought the rights to TV football from under the BBC's noses.

8. plastic – after Terry Venables had unveiled Queens Park Rangers' new all-weather pitch.

9. Wimbledon – after the Dons win the 1988 Cup Final.

10. 'Turnip' – after Graham Taylor resigns as England manager. The newspaper had cruelly called him 'Turnip' Taylor.

Rotten radio

The first radio commentary took place in 1927. It was a game between Arsenal and Sheffield United. Thinking that listeners would be totally lost without being able to see the pitch, what did the BBC do – they gave them a picture, like this!

There were two commentators, and during the game they would both talk at once. The first would describe the match, while the second would call out the section of the pitch the ball was in. This was what an article in the *Manchester Guardian* said it sounded like:

137

Since then the radio has been broadcasting football matches non-stop. Look at any big match crowd. You'll often see spectators watching the match while they listen to another on their portable radios.

Once, a whole street did this…

Foul football question:

In 1949, hundreds were locked out of the ground when non-league Yeovil played First Division Sunderland in the fourth round of the F.A. Cup. They listened to the radio commentary instead – even though portable radios hadn't been invented. How did they manage it?

Answer:

The police on crowd duty opened the doors of their patrol cars and turned their car radios up full blast so that everybody could hear!

Bite my tongue

Commentators often say some pretty daft things. Here are some from radio. Maybe radio commentators are dafter than TV commentators because they've been practising for longer…

- Tom Woodroofe, commentating during extra time of an incredibly boring 1938 F.A. Cup Final between Huddersfield and Preston, had just promised the listeners, "If they score now, I'll eat my hat" … when Preston were awarded a penalty – and scored. It was the last kick of the game.

- Mick Lowes told his listeners, "And so it's West Ham 1, Everton 0, and that's the way it stayed through half-time…"

- Denis Law gave the listeners this gem: "There is no way Ryan Giggs is another George Best. He's another Ryan Giggs."

- And Simon Mayo showed perfect timing when he said excitely, "And Lineker scored the equalizer thirteen minutes before the end. Talk about a last-minute goal!"

139

Terrible telly

Can you imagine it – no football preview programmes, no football highlights, no action replays, no live FA Cup Final or European Cup Final or World Cup Final, no action replays, no Sky Sport, no...

Well, that's how it was until just about 60 years ago. Telly wasn't terrible – it wasn't even there!

Then, very slowly, the picture took shape...

1937 The first televised football! Part of the FA Cup Final is watched by just 10,000 viewers. The following year they see the whole – and really boring! 1938 Final between Preston and Huddersfield.

1946 From now on, the F.A. Cup Final is shown live, and they're not quite as boring as 1937 either.

1955 The BBC begin showing highlights of mid-week games on a programme called Sports Special. TV football fans get some excitement, until...

140

1960 ITV televises the first-ever live game, a First Division match between Blackpool and Bolton Wanderers. It's a 0-0 bore-draw and ITV switch off again, cancelling their plans for further live games.

1964 Match of the Day begins in black-and-white, and on BBC2. It's so successful they switch it to BBC1, where it's stayed ever since...

1971 Since 1966 replays of a game's good bits have been shown. Now they can be shown really slooooowwwwly.

1992 Sky Sports pay pots of money to show Premier League matches, and they have cameras at every game. 'Interactive' TV lets fans choose which game they want to watch by pressing a button on their handset.

2008 Every game has so many cameras that nothing is missed. Good for viewers, but bad for players – they can now be punished for foul behaviour that the referee missed but the cameras spotted! Now, TV football reaches across the whole world. When the 2006 World Cup was played it was estimated that half the human race watched at least one game. Let's hope they picked the right one!

Television football has had its hiccups, though...

Foul TV tales

- In 1983, ITV began showing live matches on a Sunday afternoon – and a man murdered his girlfriend because she turned it off while he was watching.
- For the opening weeks of the 1985/86 season there was no football on TV at all because the television companies couldn't agree a fee with the football clubs. So, no pay, no play!

But for really foul football television, the only place to go is America...

Foul football on telly question:
When, in 1967, football was launched in the USA, the referee kept on stopping the match when nobody had done anything wrong. Why?

Answer:
The games were being shown on TV. When it was time for the adverts, the referee got a signal and had to stop the match! This so confused the spectators, that things were later changed. When the ball went out of play or a free kick was awarded, the referee would wave a red flag to signal that it was a good time to show the adverts. He wouldn't restart the game until they were finished.

So, there it is. From broken bones to TV breaks, football has journeyed through the years to the game you play and watch today. The rules have changed. The kit has changed. What hasn't changed is the excitement and the fun of playing football. It's still the simplest, and the greatest, game in the world.

So, grab that ball!

Get out on the pitch!

Play football – and no fouling! (Well, not when the ref's watching, anyway.)

FOUL FOOTBALL

THE BOOTIFUL GAME

SECOND HALF

For
Mike 'phantastic'
Phillips
also
Helen, Ali
Jill and Susila

INTRODUCTION

Football is the most popular sport in the world. It began in England (say the English)...

From its birth in England (if you believe the English), football has grown so much that it's now the most popular, most-played game in the world. At this minute, right now, somewhere in the world, a footballer will be scoring a goal or making a save – or committing a foul!

Yes, although the game the English invented (if you believe them) is a beautiful game it can also be pretty foul. But is it the same everywhere? Do other countries have a similar share of foul football? Is it less foul than in the place where it all began (if you believe the English). Or is it a case of foreign football being even fouler football?

This is the book to help you decide! It's got everything you need to make up your mind about where football's foulest. For instance, super stories about football folk like...

● The kindly English referee who took pity on the losing team.

● The Brazilian coach who got angry if his team didn't foul enough.

● The even fouler Uruguayan player found guilty of daylight robbery.

And, because football is about more than people, it's got a host of foul facts you need to bear in mind too, like those about...

● The foul South American crash helmet which stopped a match.

● The world competition which was better known for its foul fights than its football.

148

And you can weigh these against even fouler facts like this one about...

● The English ground which tried to swallow a footballer.

Plus, to provide even more help in your decision-making, we'll be handing out our coveted *Foul Football* awards. They'll only be presented to a select few, to those who've either done something really beautiful – or something even fouler than usual. Awards such as...

THE PITCH RAGE AWARD...

Ataulfo Valencia of Ecuadorian club Espoli, who was sent off a minute before the end of a South American cup tie against Ecuador's Barcelona in March 1996. Why? Did he commit a foul foul? No. Did Ataulfo retaliate after being 'acked? No. A trolley being used to ferry an injured player off the pitch accidentally bumped into him. Violent Valencia got a red card (and wins his even fouler award) because instead of seeing the funny side he jumped up and punched the driver!

So read on. And whatever you do, don't make up your mind before you reach the last page. That wouldn't be fair!

FOOTBALL FAR AND WIDE

Let's start by looking at how football (foul or fair) came to be played throughout the world. Did each country invent its own version? Or was the game carried to foreign shores by visitors, like a (nice) kind of football 'flu? In particular, did the game begin in England or is that a foul football fib?

Enterprising England

Let's set the facts straight. When the English say that nobody had ever played a game anything like football until they did, they're wrong. Not telling foul football fibs, just wrong. Football-like games had been played in lots of places before the English tried it. A sport similar to football was played 3,000 years ago in Japan, and Chinese writing from over 1,800 years ago talks about a football-type game played between teams from Japan and China. That's right, international matches! The game was called *Tsu Chu* which translated means football – Tsu means to kick with the foot and Chu means a ball made of leather and stuffed.

The ancient Greeks and Romans also played a game that was a bit like football – although the Greeks' version was closer to rugby because players were allowed to carry the ball. There were even organized matches in ancient Rome – with 27 men on each side!

So, football probably wasn't invented in England. But nobody can deny that what the enterprising English *did* do was to get things organized. They turned a general rough-house sport into a game with a set of rules and, in 1863, formed their own Football Association (FA) – the first in the world.

These rules were then carried across the world. Sailors and teachers and railwaymen carried them from England to countries in which they'd found work. Visitors to England heard about the rules and took them back home with them. Maybe that's why the English sing a song called: 'Rule Britannia!'

Korean kicks and Japanese jinks

In 2002, the World Cup finals were jointly held in South Korea and Japan, the first time they'd been played in Asia. And about time too, the Koreans and Japanese must have thought (although they were far too polite to say so).

As we've already seen, a football-like game was played in Japan 3,000 years ago. But the Koreans weren't new boys either. Korean history books tell of a football-like game called "chuk-kook" being played there well over 1,000 years ago!

Even the modern game had been known in Korea for well over 100 years. In 1882 the crew of a British ship called *Flying Fish* arrived in the port of Jemulpo, Incheon. Whenever the sailors came ashore they brought a football with them for a kick-about. The local lads soon joined in the fun – making such good friends with the sailors that when their ship set sail they left their football behind as a gift.

Slowly, the popularity of football grew in Korea and in 1904 it was given another big boost. This time it wasn't due to a group of sailors – but to a bunch of teachers. Deciding that their students needed something more energetic to study than maths and science, Korea's Royal Foreign Language School added football to the list of class subjects.

By the 1920s the first Korean football league had been formed. Korea was divided into north and south in 1945. In 1948, South Korea's international team competed in the London Olympic Games, and from 1956–60 the country were the undisputed Asian champions. In 1983 the South Koreans established the first professional league in Asia. Currently called the K-League, it has 15 teams. North Korea reached the World Cup quarter-final in 1966 and South Korea the semi-final in 2002. Well done, the teachers!

The arrival of modern football in Japan was confusing, to say the least. The game officially reached the country in 1873, when a game was organized at the Naval Academy in Tokyo by a British officer, Archibald Douglas, and his men. The trouble was that many of the Japanese spectators thought the match was a version of *kemari*, an ancient Japanese ball game connected with the Shinto religion!

Although the game became more popular (once people realized it *was* a game!) the Japanese Football Association wasn't formed until 1921 – and only then because something unexpected arrived to persuade them. An all-Japan Schools Soccer Tournament had just been started and the English FA had generously sent a replica of the famous FA Cup to be used as the trophy. This was something of an embarrassment because Japan didn't have a Football Association to officially receive such a splendid gift. They had to form one just for the purpose!

The following year, an amateur Japan Soccer League was established, with eight teams. Japan's football stayed strictly amateur until 1993, when the professional J-league began with such stars as England striker Gary Lineker. He's no longer playing, but the 33-team J-league is still going strong!

Born in Brazil

In 2002, Brazil became the world football champions for a record fifth time – but who can claim the credit for introducing the Brazilians to the game? There are lots of different stories. Some say it was due to British and Dutch sailors playing football matches on the beach while their ships were in port. Another gives the credit to a couple of Englishmen, named John and Hugh, who are supposed to have taught the game to the railway workers they employed.

THEY'LL NEVER GET THE HANG OF IT

The only story with real evidence to back it up, though, concerns a man with the very un-Brazilian name Charles Miller. This was because, although he was born in Brazil, his parents were English. It also explains why a not-very-cheerful Charlie was packed off to school in England. He was a lot happier when he came back, though, in 1894. He'd discovered football! Now aged 20, Miller brought with him loads of football gear and a wild enthusiasm to tell everybody about the great game he'd discovered. He did, too. Only eight years later the São Paulo league was formed. Brazil were on their way to glory!

By 1914 they had an international team. Starting the way they meant to carry on, Brazil's first-ever "international" match was a 2–1 win in a friendly match against English club side Exeter City. One of their goals that day was scored by another Brazilian with a very un-Brazilian name: Artur Friedenreich.

Friedenreich was the first great Brazilian striker. Born in 1892, he had a German father and a Brazilian mother, which qualified him to play for Brazil. After notching up that goal against Exeter, awesome Artur went on scoring for the next 20 years! Nicknamed "The Tiger", fearsome Friedenreich became the first player in the world to notch up 1000 goals. By the time his career finally ended he'd banged in a grand total of 1329!

Nifty Nigeria

Englishmen may or may not have carried their football rules to Africa, but the English influence can be seen in that continent, too. Nigeria, for example, didn't form a national football association until 1945. When they did, what was their first move? To establish their own version of the FA Cup!

Just like the English version, it began in a small way with just nine teams, all from the capital city, Lagos. Gradually other teams joined until, in 1953, a team named Kano became the first from outside Lagos to win the cup.

There have been record wins, too. Just as Preston's 26–0 beating of Hyde is still an English FA Cup record, so the Nigerian version is Warri's 18–0 whacking of Igala. Desperate losers are there, too. Between 1963 and 1974, poor Plateau were losing finalists eight times!

Of course in England nothing stops the FA Cup from taking place. But in 1973, the Nigerian FA Cup wasn't held at all so as to allow the country to concentrate on hosting the second All-Africa Games. Then there was the 1977 Cup Final, which started but didn't finish. Already 1–0 down and complaining about biased refereeing, Raccah Rovers refused to come out for the second half of their game against IICC Shooting Stars!

Nowadays Nigeria and the other African nations are steadily catching up with the rest of the footballing world. Will an African nation lift the World Cup one day? Don't bet against it. Nigeria became the first African nation to win the Olympic Games football gold medal in 1996, and won the silver at Beijing in 2008. They also won the World under-17 Cup in 2007!

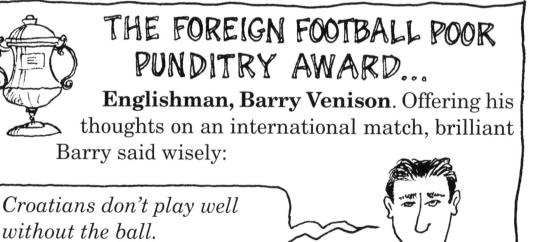

THE FOREIGN FOOTBALL POOR PUNDITRY AWARD...

Englishman, Barry Venison. Offering his thoughts on an international match, brilliant Barry said wisely:

Croatians don't play well without the ball.

The league-of-their-own quiz

The English flair for organization didn't only give football its rules, it produced ideas for organized competitions, too. Every knock-out competition in the world is based on an English invention, the FA Cup. The same goes for league competitions. The English Football League led the way in 1887–88, and soon other countries began to follow. Now, every football country has a league competition.

Here are just ten of the hundreds of leagues being played today. Match the names of each league against its host country.

LEAGUE NAME
① PREMIERSHIP (THE FIRST IN THE WORLD).
② BUNDESLIGA
③ K-LEAGUE
④ CAMPEONATO
⑤ LA LIGA
⑥ CHAMPIONNAT
⑦ PRIMERA
⑧ SERIE
⑨ J-LEAGUE
⑩ SUPERETTAN

COUNTRY
ⓐ KOREA
ⓑ ITALY
ⓒ BRAZIL
ⓓ FRANCE
ⓔ SCOTLAND
ⓕ SWEDEN
ⓖ JAPAN
ⓗ ARGENTINA
ⓘ GERMANY
ⓙ SPAIN

Answers:
1e) Scotland formed a Premier Division in 1975, 17 years before the English! **2i) 3a)** The K-League is played from spring to late autumn. **4c) 5j) 6d) 7h) 8b) 9g)** It began in 1993. **10f)**

157

Top of the world

Since 1993, every football-playing country in the world has been playing in a kind of league. Not a proper league, where each team plays every other, but a pretend league. It's called The FIFA/Coca-Cola World Ranking – because it's controlled by the world-governing body, FIFA, using sponsorship (and a huge computer program) provided by the drinks company.

The idea of the league table is to show how good (or bad) any country is at football. You could try and do the same sort of thing for the school teams in your area – if you're brave. Here's a rough idea of how you'd score ranking points whenever you play a match:

- By winning or drawing the game.
- By living where you do. The points your team scores are adjusted depending on whether the teams in your area are generally strong or generally weak.

- Pick your opponents! Winning or drawing against Manchester Marvels, a team ranked higher than you, and you earn bonus points. On the other hand, beating

158

Walsall Wobblers, a weaker team than you, won't earn you many points.

- By playing important matches. Winning a friendly kick-about behind the bike sheds counts for less than lifting the cup at a big-time, inter-schools final.

- By learning to count up to five and work out averages. Playing a hundred games a season won't give you a super-big haul of ranking points. You have to play at least five games – and the points you get for the season aren't the total, they're average.

- By trying hard year after year. The points you score in a season are mixed in with the points you've scored in the previous four seasons. So if your team once luckily beat Liverpool Legends when all their players were away from school with measles, then that historic victory will help your ranking for a while.

Phew!

The Terrific Ten

At the beginning of 2009, the highest-ranked countries in the world were:

1. Spain	2. Germany
3. Netherlands	4. Italy
5. Brazil	6. Argentina
7. Croatia	8. England
9. Russia	10. Turkey

The table changes every month, though! To check out your favourite country's current ranking, go to http://www.fifa.com/worldfootball/ranking/

Moving, Moving, Moving

In the real FIFA rankings, each year there are two awards:

- The "Team of the Year" award goes to the team whose best seven matches of the year received the greatest total points.

- The "Best Mover of the Year" award goes to the team which comes out on top after an even fouler bit of arithmetic – multiplying the points each team had at the end of the year by the points they earned during the year. This is supposed to give teams already high in the ranking the chance to win an award. (Get your teacher to prove that it does – or, if you want to be sure of getting the sums right, check it out for yourself!)

Here are five international teams. Put them in the order you think they finished in the "Best Mover" table at the end of 2008.

Rock Bottom

Which teams get the foulest headaches when they see they're propping up the rest in the rankings list? The lowest team in Europe is the world's oldest and smallest independent republic, San Marino. Not surprising really, there are only 1,200 players in the whole country! They haven't won many international matches – but then they don't expect to. As one of their coaches, Giampaolo Mazza, said:

Our aim isn't always to win, but to give the best possible account of ourselves while defending our nation's colours.

Not surprisingly, in December 2008 San Marino was ranked equal worst in the 207-country table.

161

So which teams are as bad as San Marino? Which three of the following were at the bottom in 2003 and still there five years later in 2008?

AMERICAN SAMOA:
GUAM:
MONTSERRAT:
PUERTO RICO:
TURKS AND CAICOS ILANDS:

Answer:

Since 2003, Turks and Caicos have risen to 168th and Puerto Rico to a dizzy 142nd! Still there at the bottom are Guam, American Samoa and Montserrat who - along with San Marino, Anguilla, Cook Islands and Papua New Guinea are all ranked equal 201st.

Still, don't judge Montserrat too harshly. In 1995 a large lump of the island disappeared when a volcano erupted! Not surprisingly, football on the island came to a halt — how would your team cope if its pitch and training facilities disappeared for ever under a heap of molten lava? The Montserratians are made of tough stuff, though. A five-team league restarted in 2000 and improving their world ranking is their next target. Well, at least it can't get any worse!

CLUB COMPENDIUM

Every football-playing country has its big clubs whose names are known all over the world. Never forget, though that every big club was once a little club with an urge to grow.

In England, for example, you can bet that when the Newton Heath (Lancashire and Yorkshire Railway) Football Club was formed in 1878, at least one of its founders would lie in bed every night dreaming that their team would one day grow into a world-famous team called – oh, Manchester United, say. (Which they did!)

Likewise you can be sure that when a group of bomb-making workers got together in 1886 and called their team Dial Square FC, at least one of them hoped that they'd explode into a league and cup double-winning side with a name like – say, Arsenal. (Which they did!)

Here's a grower's guide to how some of the world's top club sides began.

I've had this great idea...

Ajax (Holland)

Dutch enthusiast Han Dade was the owner of what, in 1883, was a rare article – a real leather football! Not surprisingly, he was popular with his mates. So when Han suggested they form a football club in 1900 he wasn't short of players – at least, not until Han's rules began to bite. Determined Dade ensured that Ajax club members played fair not foul by ruling that they could be fined for such things as:

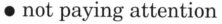

- not telling the captain they were going to be absent
- "inappropriate words or acts" (that is, foul language or foul play)
- not paying attention

The players obviously said "fair enough", because Ajax went on to become not only the most famous team in Holland, but also the team with the reputation for being the fairest.

Barcelona (Spain)

Who says footballers only look at the pictures in the newspapers? If the residents of Barcelona hadn't been able to read, their club might never have been formed. That's because the way Swiss businessman Hans Gamper set about finding players for a new team was to put an advert in a local sports magazine. This was on 22 October 1899, and just one month later a meeting was held to set up the club – with an English president, Gualteri Wild. Three years later Barcelona reached the Spanish Cup final.

Bayern Munich (Germany)

Another man with an English name gets the credit for setting up the top German club. Franz John already played for a club called MTV 1879 but he wasn't happy. On 27 February 1900, John called a meeting of other miserable MTV-men at a restaurant. During their meal, the gathering carved out plans to set up a new club called FC Bayern. Their move certainly served up a nasty surprise for their old club, MTV. Bayern's first match was against Franz John's former team and they ran out 7–1 winners!

Boca Juniors (Argentina)

Pat MacCarthy left his native Ireland on a ship, which ended up in the Argentine port of La Boca, in Buenos Aires. He found he wasn't alone. He was surrounded not only by fellow Irish immigrants, but by Italians as well, all looking for work. It wasn't long before they were soon labouring side by side, loading and unloading ships, but they didn't speak the same language – at least, not until they all began kicking a football around during their rest periods. Then they understood each other! In 1905, the work-mates formed Boca Juniors FC, and the club has been supported as "the team of the workers" ever since.

Glasgow Celtic (Scotland)

Celtic were formed in 1887 thanks to another Irishman, by the name of Walfrid. But was "Walfrid" **a)** his first name, or **b)** his second name?

In the nineteenth-century, Scotland was the destination for thousands of Irish immigrants forced by famine to leave their homeland to try and find work in Glasgow's factories and shipyards. Unfortunately there simply weren't enough jobs to go round, so Brother Walfrid had the idea of starting a football club. He thought it would give his poor parishioners in the Parkhead area an interest

On 28 May 1888, Celtic played their first game. A crowd of 2,000 turned up to see them win 5–2 in a friendly against a team from the other end of the city. Their name? Rangers.

THE IT'S-ONLY-FAIR-TO-LET-HIM-IN-FOR-NOTHING AWARD...

Brother Walfrid. In recognition of the part he played in setting up the club, Brother Walfrid (and any other Catholic priest) was allowed in to watch Celtic's home matches free – a tradition that was maintained for over 100 years.

Dynamo Kiev (Ukraine)

In terms of age, Dynamo Kiev are youngsters. They weren't founded until 1927. At the time, Ukraine was part of the Soviet Union and the usual thing was for sports teams to represent the organizations that their players worked for – which is how Dynamo Kiev came into being. The Soviet Union was a massive country with an equally massive police force to keep foul behaviour under control – and Dynamo were their team. Yes, the Kiev kickers wore police boots for work and football boots for play!

AC Milan (Italy)

For a top Italian football club, AC Milan was founded in a curious way. Three Englishmen (not Italian men) decided over a glass of beer (not wine) to form a ... cricket (not football) club!

This happened in December 1899 when – believe it or not – cricket was much more popular than football. The members' aim for the Milan Cricket and Football Club was to play cricket as much as possible and try to encourage others to take up football.

They succeeded! You'd have to look very hard to find any cricket balls at a Milan match nowadays.

Panathanaikos (Greece)

This top Greek team had no need to look for either a doctor or a trainer after they were formed (as the Athens Football Club) by George Calafatis in 1908. Clever Calafatis could cope with both fouls and fitness because he'd studied medicine at the University of Athens and gymnastics at the Academy of Gymnastics. He was talented enough to have been an Olympic athlete but his great love was football. He wasn't bad at that, either. His team's first official match was a 9–0 victory, with goal-grabber George hitting a hat trick!

Penarol (Uruguay)

Not every club has been *totally* grateful to its founders – but in Penarol's case it's understandable. Formed by workers at the British-owned Central Urugauyan Railway company in 1891, they started life with the mouthful of a name:

CENTRAL URUGUAYAN RAILWAY CRICKET CLUB

But by 1913 two things had happened. Football fanaticism had taken hold, and the British had begun to leave the country to work elsewhere. The Central Uruguayan Railway was handed over to the Urugayans. As fast as a flying winger the club changed its name to Penarol, after the district in which the railway offices were based.

The Thingummy FC Quiz

Penarol are just one of many clubs (like Manchester United and Arsenal) whose names have changed in some way since they were founded. Use this set of well-known club names to replace the word THINGUMMY in the facts that follow.

a) THINGUMMY are the sports club of the electronics company, Philips.

b) Annoyed that their club was refusing to accept foreign players as well as the home-grown variety, a group of rebels broke away to form THINGUMMY.

c) They got their name because one of the club's founders saw THINGUMMY printed on the side of a container that had just been unloaded from a ship.

d) THINGUMMY was copied! It was the name of an English rugby club of the time.

e) You can't call your team THINGUMMY unless you've got supporters in high places – or, rather, high palaces!

f) This team was formed by a group of young students so it made sense for them to choose the name THINGUMMY.

g) English spelling wasn't the strong point of the founders of this team: their first attempt at a club name was "Footh-ball Club THINGUMMY".

Answers:

a) PSV Eindhoven. The PSV stands for Philips Sport Vereniging – that is, Philips Sports Club. They're basically a works team who've managed to win the European Cup!

b) Internazionale. – where "internazionale" means "international". It happened in 1908, nine years after the Milan Cricket and Football Club was formed. In other words, Inter Milan is the son of AC Milan! They're friends now, though – the two clubs even share a ground. For a while, though, you wouldn't have known that Inter were a Milanese team. During the 1930s the Italian government forced them to change their name to "Ambrosiana"!

c) River Plate. The club (like its great rivals, Boca

Junior) was founded by immigrant dockworkers who were attracted to the game by seeing English sailors having a kick-about. That's how the name was chosen. One of the new team's players saw the name "River Plate" on the side of a ship's container and thought it would be a really dishy name for a football team!

d) Glasgow Rangers. The team was started in 1873 by three young Scots after seeing a group playing a game of football on Glasgow Green. It was one of these three, a Moses McNeil, who came up with the name "Rangers" – he'd seen it used as a team name in a book about English rugby.

e) Real Madrid. The team began life as plain old Madrid FC in March, 1902. They stayed that way until 29 June 1920. That was the day their biggest fan, King Alfonso XIII, gave them permission to stick the word "Real" (Spanish for "Royal") on the front.

f) Juventus. Legend has it that the club began life on a bench in Re Umberto Avenue, Turin. That's where, in 1897, a group of college students decided that starting their own football club would give them something interesting to do (obviously they didn't fancy studying!) Being young and Italian, they knew that the Latin word for young was "Juventus". The club was originally called Sports Club Juventus. Two years later the name was changed to Football Club Juventus.

g) Ajax. The dodgy spellers began by calling their team "Union", only to change it to "Footh-Ball Club Ajax". When Ajax lost the ground they played their footh-ball on, it gave the organisers a chance to put matters right. At a crisis meeting in a café on 18 March 1900, the club was re-formed as a properly spelt "Football Club Ajax".

THE POSSIBLY FOULER AND DEFINITELY MADDER NAME FOR A NEW FOOTBALL TEAM AWARD...

Colo Colo of Chile. The club was formed by five players who'd had a big argument with their previous club, Magallanes FC, and were still feeling angry about things – hence their choice of "Colo Colo". It's the Chilean nickname for a wild cat!

172

Shirt Tales

Anybody wanting to start up a new team nowadays would have to spend ages simply discussing the details of what kind of football shirts they were going to wear! They'd have to worry about what size letters to have for the players' names, where their sponsor's logo was going to go, whether the shirts were going to have short sleeves or long sleeves, was the team's name going to be stitched on to the collar or the tail, or the collar *and* the tail ... and so on. There are so many possibilities they'd do well to find time to actually play a match!

But that's now. In football's early days life was much simpler. A football shirt didn't always look that different to a normal shirt, except that you didn't wear a tie with it.

WE MAY BE USELESS BUT NOBODY CAN SAY WE'RE NOT SMARTLY TURNED OUT!

Add a club badge, and you were there. Spanish giants Barcelona, for example, have played in their famous blue and claret colours since day one. But even they couldn't decide what to have as a club crest. So they decided to hold a competition – and the badge on their shirts today is the same design which won that competition. It was the entry of a Barcelona supporter named ... anonymous. To this day nobody knows who that competition winner was.

Feeling cross?

Italian club AC Milan don't have the same problem. They know exactly who designed the badge on their famous red-and-black striped shirts. It was one of their founders, Herbert Kilpin – a patriotic Englishman. At that time, most English club badges showed England's flag, the Cross of St George, as part of their design. Kilpin didn't see anything at all foul about copying them – so he did. That is why, to this day, AC Milan's badge includes that old red cross on a white background.

That's not to say the club are stuck in the past, though. In many ways AC Milan's shirts have been ahead of their time. In 1981 the club were the first to print their player's names on the back of the shirts. They were also the first to introduce a sponsor's name.

Seeing Red

Sparta Prague of the Czech Republic were another club who thought English football shirts were anything but foul – and even if they did, the design they started with was even fouler. When the club was formed in 1893, Sparta played their early games wearing black shirts with a large "S" for "Sparta" on the front.

This changed in 1906. Their club president made a trip to England and while there he was taken to see one of Arsenal's league matches. So impressed was he by the club's red shirts he decided there and then that as far as his own team's kit was concerned it was going to be "S" for "Scrap". When he got back home Sparta changed to the red shirts they still wear.

All White!

Copying colours was seen as a perfectly fair thing to do, in fact. For a club to copy another's colours was seen as a mark of respect.

That was Real Madrid's argument, anyway. Their founders settled on a strip of white shirts and white shorts because they wanted to be just like a team from London called Corinthians. Yes, an English team! The Corinthians were a world-famous amateur team who regularly provided over half England's players in the 1890s and 1900s. What's more, no side played fairer football. If a Corinthians defender ever gave away a penalty, their goalkeeper would refuse to try and save the kick.

175

Wrong? Right!

Italian club Juventus were another who changed their shirts because of the English influence. The difference in their case was that it happened by mistake!

After their formation in 1900, the team had started out wearing pretty pink shirts. Three years later they must have been wearing thin, because the decision was taken to order a new set from the manufacturers in England. Back came the parcel – only for the club to discover that they'd been sent the wrong set. Instead of the colour Juventus had ordered, the shirt-makers had sent a set intended for the English club, Notts County – in black-and-white stripes.

Were the shirt-makers left pink with embarrassment? No, because Juventus didn't complain. They liked the stripes so much they adopted them at once and have been ordering them ever since!

So it looks like the English style of football shirt was regarded as a fair bet. It certainly was if you compare it to those worn by Scottish team Clyde FC in 1919.

The First World War had just ended and money was in short supply; Clyde didn't have the cash to splash out on a smart new set of shirts. All they could afford were the kind of shirts on special offer at their local army-surplus store. In went their order – and out ran the Clyde players for their next match in colours of foul sludge-brown khaki.

THE EVEN FOULER SHIRTS AWARD...

Ajax Cape Town (South Africa) whose shirts were foul enough to get them expelled from the South African Super League in October 2003. The rules said that every club had to wear shirts carrying the name of the league's sponsor, the Japanese car manufacturer Toyota. After failing to do this three times, Ajax were driven out of the league. They would have been champions.

Playing fair or playing foul?

Every famous top club had to rise from being an unknown bottom club. Here are some that managed to do just that – but was it by fair means or foul?

1 Moscow Dynamo achieved fame as the first Russian club to venture abroad when they travelled to Britain in 1945. Did the team go back home with a reputation for being **fair or foul?**

THIS IS HIS FIRST TIME ABROAD!

2 In 1992, French team Olympique Marseille were another side with money to spend. They won the French championship, then went on to win the European Cup. But had they used **fair means or foul?**

3 In the 1950s Columbian club Millonarios had a brief spell of fame by offering big money to players willing to join them. Many stars did just that and Millonarios' blue-shirted players danced round the opposition so well that they were nicknamed "the blue ballet". But were Millonarios regarded as **fair or foul?**

4 Nacional of Uruguay must hold the record for the quickest rise to top level. Formed in 1899, they'd become good enough just four years later to be sent out to represent their country. Did they do it by **fair means or foul?**

5 Dynamo Kiev were another team which became good enough to represent their country. In the qualifying competition for the 1976 European Championships, the then USSR players (Kiev is now in Ukraine) were almost all from Dynamo. What's more, as they were officially amateurs, the same players became the USSR's football team for the Olympic Games as well! But when they were formed in 1927, were Dynamo thought of as a **fair team or foul?**

Answers:

1 Fair Even though Dynamo gave their opponents a hard time – they drew with Chelsea (3-3) and Rangers (2-2), and beat Arsenal (4–3) and Cardiff (10–1!) – they impressed all who saw them with their fair play and teamwork. What's more, before each game every Dynamo player presented his opposite number with a lovely bunch of flowers!

2 Foul It was proved that Marseille had used some of their money to bribe opposition teams not to try against them. Once the truth came out Marseille were fined, relegated – and eventually went bust.

3 Foul Millonarios were members of a Columbian "pirate" league – that is, a league which wasn't linked to an official Football Association. This meant that no team outside Columbia was allowed to play them.

4 Fair And their performance on that occasion was pretty good too. They won their match, beating deadly rivals Argentina 3–2!

5 Foul (That's what crooks thought, anyway.) Russian football teams were made up of workers who had the same sort of job during the day and Dynamo Kiev's players were all policemen! They weren't particularly good at football, either. Dynamo spent their first few seasons being overrun by the railway workers of Lokomotiv Kiev. In other words, the team that became the USSR's finest were once not even the best in Kiev!

The matches of death

Dynamo Kiev are at the centre of a story about a newly formed team which is probably part-true and part-legend – but definitely completely amazing. The story concerns the Kiev side and opponents who proved to be even fouler than anybody could imagine...

HERE ARE THE FACTS NOBODY DOUBTS:

IN AUGUST 1942, AS THE SECOND WORLD WAR SPREAD DRAMATICALLY, KIEV WAS CAPTURED BY THE GERMAN FORCES...

MANY OF THE KIEV PLAYERS (BOTH DYNAMO AND LOKOMOTIV) WERE TRAPPED...

THEY SPENT THEIR DAYS WORKING IN A KIEV BAKERY...

DURING THIS TIME THEY BEGAN PLAYING TOGETHER FOR A NEW FOOTBALL TEAM. IT WAS CALLED START F.C.

NOW WE START (HO·HO!) GETTING INTO THE DOUBTFUL BITS...

SOME SAY THE KIEV PLAYERS FORMED START FC THEMSELVES; OTHERS, THAT THEY WERE MADE TO DO IT BY THE GERMAN FORCES.

SOME SAY THAT START FC ARRANGED MATCHES FOR THEMSELVES; OTHERS THAT THE GERMAN FORCES MADE THEM PLAY VARIOUS TOP TEAMS THEY BROUGHT IN FROM GERMANY AND OTHER COUNTRIES THEY'D CAPTURED.

BACK TO PARTS OF THE STORY THAT EVERYBODY IS AGREED ON:

EVEN THOUGH THE KIEV PLAYERS WERE UNFIT AND HUNGRY, THE PART-TIME BAKERS ALWAYS ROSE TO THE OCCASION. THEY WON EVERY GAME THEY PLAYED.

SEEING THIS, THE SPIRITS OF THE KIEV PEOPLE ROSE AS WELL. THE TEAM WAS GIVING THEM REASON TO SMILE AGAIN.

182

IT'S BACK TO THE DOUBTFUL BITS NOW. AND GET YOUR HANDKERCHIEFS READY...

IT'S SAID THAT START FC'S SUCCESSES MADE THEIR CAPTORS ANGRY - SO ANGRY THAT THEY DECIDED TO BRING IN THE BEST TEAM THEY POSSIBLY COULD. PACKED WITH GERMANY'S BEST PLAYERS, THEY WOULD CRUSH KIEV AND SHOW THEM WHO WAS BOSS.

IT'S SAID THAT THE START TEAM WERE TOLD THAT IF THEY WON THIS MATCH THEY WOULD BECOME NON-STARTERS IN THE FUTURE; THEY'D NEVER PLAY AGAIN... BECAUSE THEY'D BE DEAD.

IT'S SAID THAT THE GAME WAS PLAYED... AND THAT TO THE JOY OF THE KIEV PEOPLE, START FC FINISHED AS THEY'D STARTED AND WON YET AGAIN.

IT'S SAID THAT THE CAPTORS WERE TRUE TO THEIR WORD. ONE BY ONE THE KIEV STARS WERE TRANSFERRED FROM THE BAKERY TO CONCENTRATION CAMPS... AND NEVER CAME OUT.

EVEN FOULER FOOTBALLERS

It doesn't matter where you go, football – like all other professions – has its fair share of foul players and even fouler teams. Check out these tales to discover the sort of things they get up to. (But do *not* try them when you're playing for the school side!)

Daylight robbery

It's not unknown for teams to say their opponents have stolen the game with a last-minute goal. But it's quite unusual to have a game end with a player actually arrested for being a thief!

It happened in 1991, as the top Uruguayan teams Penarol and Nacional were doing battle. As usual Dely Valdez, Nacional's striker, was wearing the collection of valuable gold necklaces he was famous for. Against him was Penarol defender Goncalves. At one point during the match, as the two players were in a tussle near the corner flag, Goncalves whipped off one of Valdez' necklaces and hid it in his football sock. Unfortunately for the Penarol plunderer, although dozy Dely didn't spot that he was a necklace short, the TV cameras covering the match certainly did. The moment the teams left the pitch, Goncalves was arrested!

184

Was it gaol for Goncalves? No – he gave the necklace back and charges were dropped.

Brazilian goalkeeper Fabio Costa, on the other hand, made no attempt to hide what he'd stolen during a league match between his club Vitoria and Atletico Mineiro. In protest at having a penalty awarded against him, he took ... the match ball! When the Atletico players tried to get it back to get on with the game Fabio the Grabio beat them off with karate kicks. A big brawl followed until, after a full ten minutes, the ball was prised from Costa's clutches and the game restarted.

You're so rude!

Footballers who show off their bits (naughty or otherwise) are frowned on nowadays. Referees can shout

"foul" and give a player a yellow card for whipping his shirt off in celebration – or for lifting it up to reveal a message underneath.

Even in the days when it wasn't a crime, not everybody thought that shirt-throwing was a clever thing to do. In 1997, after Celtic's Portuguese player Jorge Cadete threw his dirty shirt into the crowd at the end of a match, his manager Tommy Burns said:

That sort of behaviour doesn't wash with me!

A far fouler example from Brazil in 1997 showed that the opposite can occur. Paulo Mata, coach of Brazilian league side Lapertuna, showed his players how *not* to behave. Upset that three of his players had been sent off in the closing minutes of a 3–2 defeat by Vasco da Gama, Mata raced on to the field and waggled his bare bum at the referee!

Spanish club Alfacar didn't have just one player removing an item of kit – the whole team did it. What's more, they didn't stop with their shirts. They kept going until they'd removed everything else as well!

It wasn't foul play this time, though. On the contrary, it was all in a good cause. It happened in 1998, with the club desperately in need of money. So to raise funds the players came up with the idea of doing – a striptease act! They booked their town's biggest disco and started practising.

When it came to the big night, though, only 13 of the 21-strong squad of players joined the line-up. The other eight were left out because their horrified wives and girlfriends wouldn't let them take part!

Liverpool and England star Kevin Keegan also did a striptease act that wasn't foul. It wasn't even intentional. He was on the substitutes bench for England's vital World Cup qualifying match against Poland in October 1973. With England needing to win, but only drawing 1–1, Keegan was desperate to get on the pitch. So when, with just a few minutes to go, manager Sir Alf Ramsey said, "Kevin, get ready!" he didn't waste any time. He leapt to his feet while Liverpool team mate Ray Clemence pulled off his tracksuit trousers ... and, in his haste, Keegan's shorts ... and undies!

The worst was yet to come. There were two Kevins on the bench that night and Ramsey had been calling for the other one, Kevin Hector of Derby County. While Keegan hastily covered himself up again Hector went on. He just failed to score, the match ended 1–1, England went out of the World Cup and Ramsey was sacked. A bad night all round.

Insufficient effort

Nothing makes a fan more mad than the suspicion that the footballers he's paying to watch aren't playing fair and trying their hardest. In England, a Sheffield Wednesday fan named Bob Montgomerie was so disgusted with his team's pathetic performance in losing an FA Cup 6th round replay 5–1 to Southampton in 1984 that he took them to court! Perhaps remembering that when Queen Victoria died in 1901 all football grounds had been closed because they were thought of as "places of entertainment", Montgomerie said he'd paid for his ticket expecting to be entertained – and the Sheffield Wednesday players hadn't tried to do that at all! This, he argued, meant the club had obtained his money under false pretences. Sadly the judge didn't agree.

187

In 1997 a VIP fan in an even fouler mood was Kamal al-Ganzuri, Egypt's prime minister. After his country's international team surprisingly lost a World Cup qualifying match to tiny Ghana, crafty Kamal decided that it would do the posing players good if they didn't see their pictures on the back pages of the daily newspapers for a while. So he personally asked editors not to publish reports of Egypt's matches for the next 50 days.

Did al-G's antics pay off? No. The editors refused to do what he'd asked – and, to make matters worse, splashed the story all over their *front* pages as well!

Trying hard isn't a lot of good if a footballer is using drugs to make it happen. It's been claimed that in 1978, foul Eastern European players took drugs under the orders of their even fouler military governments.

Players have their pee tested to detect this sort of dirty trick, of course, so to get away with it other people's pee was given to the testers instead. What made the testers think something dodgy was going on? The test on the pee, which was supposed to have come from one powerful player, showed that he was expecting a baby!

IS KLAUS PUTTING ON WEIGHT?

Sometimes footballers just can't win. If they don't try hard they get shouted at – but, in one player's case, trying too hard got him sacked!

In 2002, South Korean striker Ahn Jung-hwan played for Italian club, Perugia. At least he did until Japan surprisingly knocked Italy out of the 2002 World Cup finals, and Perugia's chairman Luciano Gaucci decided that Ahn should be gahn. Why? Because it had been action-man Ahn who'd won the match for Japan with an extra-time golden goal.

Sinister spells

Sometimes teams don't worry so much about avoiding foul play as avoiding foul luck. Either they'll try to make sure they don't suffer any – or somebody will claim to have tried on their behalf.

England's star foul-luck-foiler is a man named Uri Geller, whose special claim to fame is his uncanny ability to bend spoons. Useful Uri claimed to have helped hosts England reach the semi-finals of the European Championships in 1996. How? By sprinkling magic crystals at various places in Wembley Stadium. So why hadn't England gone all the way and won the title? Because, said Geller, he wasn't allowed in to sprinkle on the pitch before their match against Germany – and that's why England had lost on a penalty shoot-out.

189

Two years later, before England headed off to France for the 1998 World Cup finals, Uri Geller was back "helping" again. This time he said he'd energized the World Cup trophy itself, filling it full of good luck for the England team. Unfortunately he'd have done better to energize the England team. They were beaten by Argentina in another penalty shoot-out!

England may not have been helped by Uri Geller's attempt to "bend" the rules, but in Kenya some fans thought their opponents were trying an even fouler trick – with a bottle of water!

In 1995, regional league side Chememil were accused of practising juju (witchcraft) on their opponents, Agro-Chemical. How? By placing a bottle of water in the back of their goal. (Yes, water. Not even a bottle of evil spirits!)

They thought it had been charmed by an unfriendly witch doctor – a suspicion that was reinforced when Chemelil flatly refused to remove the bottle. That really convinced the Agro fans that something was going on and they stormed the pitch to cause some agro. The match was held up for half an hour as battle raged!

Similar suspicions of foul play also caused problems at an African Champions League match in 1998. When Mozambique team Ferroviaro missed a penalty against Zimbabwean side Dynamos, the home team were pretty sure they knew why. No, it wasn't because Ferroviaro had a pathetic penalty-taker, but that a spare set of goalkeeping gloves had been left beside one post of Dynamos' goal.

First a Ferroviaro player was booked for snatching the gloves to check them for magic charms. Then a voice began accusing the Dynamos' goalkeeper of being a witch doctor – over the ground's tannoy system! Not surprisingly there was a small riot between home fans and the police as the pitch was invaded and the offending gloves stolen.

Finally, there's the story of Racing Club of Argentina, who didn't simply think that one particular team were trying nasty tricks on them. Back in 1998 they were convinced that the whole underworld had it in for them and that their 32-year run of failure to win the Argentine Championship was due to evil spirits haunting their ground.

So they held a special torchlight ceremony. All their fans were told to turn up wearing their holiest (not hole-iest!) white. They then held a religious service. After that the Racing team came out to play a friendly match and prove that all was now well. It wasn't. Racing lost the match 2–0!

The porkie-pies quiz

In the summer of 2003, England star David Beckham moved from Manchester United to Real Madrid for £25 million. It was a move that both sides had been talking about for months. But had they been telling the truth? Here are just ten quotes from that period. Replace PORKIE-PIE* in each quote with the correct word from this list:

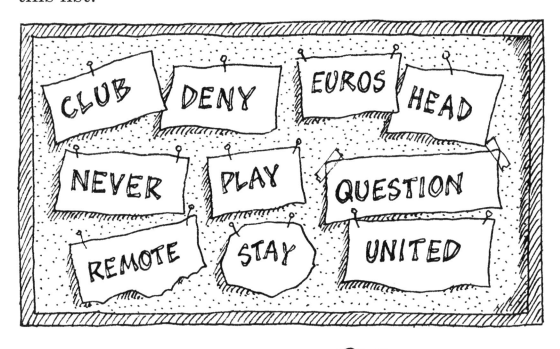

(a) THE POSSIBILITY HE WILL ONE DAY PLAY FOR REAL MADRID IS VERY PORKIE-PIE – REAL MADRID'S MANAGING DIRECTOR, JOHN VALDANO, MARCH 27.

(b) IT IS TOTALLY OUT OF THE PORKIE-PIE, THERE IS NO WAY WE WOULD SELL HIM, OR ANY OF OUR BEST PLAYERS– MANCHESTER UNITED MANAGER, SIR ALEX FERGUSON, APRIL 4.

*In Cockney rhyming slang a "porkie-pie" is a lie.

(c) BECKS TO PORKIE-PIE – DAILY MAIL NEWSPAPER HEADLINE, APRIL 7.

(d) IT HAS NOT ENTERED THE PORKIE-PIE OF ANYONE AT REAL MADRID THAT BECKHAM COULD PLAY FOR REAL MADRID NEXT SEASON – REAL MADRID PRESIDENT FLORENTINO PEREZ, APRIL 6.

(e) WE CAN CATEGORICALLY PORKIE-PIE THAT ANY DEAL IS IN PLACE TO SELL DAVID BECKHAM TO REAL MADRID– MANCHESTER UNITED STATEMENT, APRIL 12.

(f) PORKIE-PIE, PORKIE-PIE, PORKIE-PIE, PORKIE-PIE NOTHING, PORKIE-PIE, PORKIE-PIE, PORKIE-PIE, PORKIE-PIE. NOT NOW. NOT EVER. REAL MADRID PRESIDENT FLORENTINO PEREZ, APRIL 29. (SAME WORD EVERY TIME!)

(g) I WANT TO STAY AT PORKIE-PIE – DAVID BECKHAM, MAY 6.

(h) I'D RATHER JACK IT IN THAN LEAVE UNITED. THEY'RE THE ONLY TEAM I'VE EVER WANTED TO PORKIE-PIE FOR – DAVID BECKHAM, THE NEWS OF THE WORLD NEWSPAPER, JUNE 15.

i) MANCHESTER UNITED TODAY REACHED AGREEMENT FOR THE TRANSFER OF DAVID BECKHAM TO REAL MADRID FOR A FEE OF 35 MILLION PORKIE-PIE. – STATEMENT RELEASED BY MANCHESTER UNITED, JUNE 17.

j) I KNOW THAT I WOULD ALWAYS REGRET IT LATER IN LIFE IF I HAD TURNED DOWN THE CHANCE TO PLAY AT ANOTHER GREAT PORKIE-PIE LIKE REAL MADRID. DAVID BECKHAM, JUNE 17.

Answers:
a) remote; b) question; c) stay; d) head; e) deny; f) never; g) United; h) play; i) euros; j) club.

So who was telling foul fibs? The player? The two clubs? Or were the newspapers which printed it all telling even fouler fibs? You'll have to decide for yourselves – but in future bear in mind this Foul Football award winner...

THE VERY TRUE AWARD...

Ivan Esar, who wasn't a footballer or a reporter, but an American writer. In 1943 he published what he called his *Comic Dictionary*. In it he provided the definition: *Truth – the only thing that you cannot add to without subtracting from.*

CONTINENTAL COMPETITIONS

If you need proof that football is the most widespread game in the world you need look no further than all the international competitions that exist nowadays. Do the English claim the credit for inventing international games too? Of course! Well ... together with Scotland, Wales and Northern Ireland they do.

The four countries were the first to play each other in a competition. Called the Home International Championship, it began way back in the 1883–84 season and lasted for 101 years. By then bigger competitions had become more important. The biggest, of course, is the World Cup which takes place every four years. Other major competitions are the European Championship, the African Nations Cup and the South American Championship. But these are all for international teams.

For club sides there are even more international competitions. What are they? Where are they? Did they begin in England, too? Find out with this tournament timeline:

1927 The Mitropa Cup begins. It's the first international club competition in the world – and England aren't involved! It's played for by the champion clubs of Austria, Czechoslovakia, Hungary, Italy, Romania, Switzerland and Yugoslavia.

1949 The Latin Cup begins. It isn't to discover which club has the most footballers who can speak Latin (there'd have been too many 0–0 draws!), but a competition between the league champions of France, Spain, Italy and Portugal. It lasts until 1957.

1955 The European FA, UEFA (which stands for *Union des Associations Europeenes de Football*) are dithering over whether or not a competition could be started to include all the champion clubs in Europe. After quite a bit of prompting (see next section) they do just that – and call the competition the European Champion Clubs' Cup.

1959 The International Football Association, FIFA (it actually stands for *Federation Internationale de Football Asociation),* invent the ultimate club competition, the World Club Cup. The idea is that it will be an annual match between the winners of the European Champion Clubs' Cup and the South American champions. The only problem is that South America don't have a champions' cup. So they invent one, quick!

196

1960 The Liberty Cup, known in Spanish as the *Copa Libertadores da America* begins as a competition to discover the South American club champions. It's organized by the Confederacion Sudamerica de Futbol (known by the abbreviation CONMEBOL – work that one out if you can!).

1960 Another European club competition begins, the Intertoto Cup, it's a summer competition. Why? Because the clubs want it that way? No – because it's said that football fans want some proper matches to bet on during the summer months! The Intertoto Cup lasted until 2008.

1964 The African FC Champions Cup begins. Organized by the Confederation Africaine de Football (CAF) it starts out as a knockout tournament between champion clubs. Nowadays it's run as a league competition.

1987 The Oceania Clubs Championship begins, run by the Oceania Football Confederation (OFC) for club teams in the southern hemisphere. Nowadays the competition is played every two years as a tournament lasting about two weeks.

1988–1999 Clubs tournaments multiply like mad. They include tournaments like the African Cup Winners Cup for knockout cup champions and the UEFA Cup – a competition for best-performing European league sides who haven't qualified for any other competition and want to go in for one!

2000 FIFA launches what it hopes will be the ultimate club competition for the winners of each and every federation's championships. It's called the World Club Championships and is held for the first time in Brazil. It's won by Corinthians of Brazil. Europe's champions are a team from England, called Manchester United. They're knocked out at the group stages, but simply by taking part they're once again leading the way...

2001-09 No seriously new competitions at all. There's no time to play them!

We all follow Man Utd!

Since 1994, Europe's top club competition has been known as the European Champions League or "Champions League" for short. Between 1955, when it began, and 1993 it was known as the European Cup. All of which goes to show that it's perfectly possible for even the most fanatical fans to get something totally wrong for 50 years – because the proper name for Europe's top competition has always been, and still is, the European Champion Clubs' Cup!

So how did anybody know who were the top European team before this competition began (whatever it was called)? The answer is, they didn't. Although the Mitropa Cup had been running for nearly 30 years, it didn't cover all the teams in Europe. As a result, any country could claim their champions were the best. And, in 1955, the English newspapers were doing just that for the Football League champions, Wolverhampton Wanderers. Were they believed? Not by one French newspaper, they weren't...

Daily Boast...

They've just hammered Honved of Hungary and Honved's best players play for Hungary who are the best country in the world...

L'EQUIPE

But they LOST the 1954 World Cup Final to West Germany!

Daily Boast...

Don't matter about that. They beat England 6-3 and 7-1 in 1953, so they must be the best country.

And that makes Wolves the club champions of the world!

L'EQUIPE

What about EUROPE?

Daily Boast...

Er... if Europe's in the world, YEAH!

L'EQUIPE

There's only one way to settle this, you know.

Daily Boast...

RIGHT!

YOU JUST SAY OUI!

L'EQUIPE

NON! WE HAVE A COMPETITION!

And that's how the European Cup began. Annoyed about British newspapers claiming that the English champions, Wolverhampton Wanderers, were the best club side in the world, the French newspaper *L'Equipe* set up a

200

meeting with Europe's top sides and suggested a knockout competition to decide which of them really was the best. Everybody said yes, UEFA agreed to run it – and the competition kicked off!

THE NOT-YET-GOOD-ENOUGH BEST CLUB IN THE WORLD AWARD...

Wolverhampton Wanderers. Ironically Wolves didn't qualify for the first European Champion Clubs' Cup competition – because by the time it began they were no longer league champions! When Wolves qualified next, in 1959, they were knocked out in the first round. They did better a year later, reaching the quarter-finals before losing 9–2 on aggregate to Barcelona. But they haven't won it yet or qualified for it again.

Chelsea were the team who'd beaten Wolves to the 1954–55 English league title. How many games did Chelsea lose in that first season of European Cup games? Was it...

Answer: a) But the only reason they didn't lose any was because they didn't play any! Even though they'd qualified, Chelsea decided not to take part. They'd been talked out of it by the organizers of the Football League who'd said the competition would mean them having to play too many games.

So it was left for Manchester United to show English clubs the way. A year later, after winning the 1955–56 league title, they entered the 1956–57 competition. This was in spite of them being advised, just like Chelsea, not to take part. United manager Matt Busby ignored the advice, saying:

The Continental challenge should be met, not avoided.

In their first game his team didn't just meet the challenge, they trampled all over it. They won their first home tie 10–0! The unlucky opponents were Anderlecht of Belgium. United could have won by more but the players spent the last part of the game trying, unsuccessfully, to make a goal for winger David Pegg who was the only outfield player not to score!

What made the victory even more spectacular was that the "home" match hadn't been played at United's own ground, Old Trafford, but at Maine Road, the ground of their local rivals Manchester City. Competition rules said that matches had to be played under decent floodlights and in 1955 Old Trafford didn't have any! They were still being constructed.

Those weren't the days of pampered stars, either. An away tie in Spain against Atletico Bilbao was played in thick snow. Worse, after losing 5–3, the United players then had to help shovel snow from the airport runway so that their aeroplane could take off and get them home! They'd all thawed out by the second leg, though, winning 3–0 to take the tie 6–5 on aggregate.

United had reached the semi-final. Now they met another Spanish team – and were beaten 3–1 in the first leg match. Back they came for the return leg under the (now built) Old Trafford floodlights. In a ding-dong game, Manchester United were held to a 2–2 draw, which meant they were out of the competition 5–3 on aggregate.

They'd been beaten by the most famous team that European club competition has ever seen: Real Madrid.

White hot – Real Madrid

Real Madrid had come a long way since their club offices had been the back room of a shop and they'd changed into their famous white shirts in a tavern. By 1955 they were the top team in Spain. For the next five years nobody could argue that they were also the top team in Europe. Why not? Because marvellous Madrid won the competition every single year! Here's their record:

1955-56: Beat Reims (France) 4-3

1956-57: Beat Horentina (Italy) 2-0

1957-58: Beat AC Milan (Italy) 3-2

1958-59: Beat Reims (France) 2-0

Then, in 1959–60, Real won their way through to their fifth final in a row.

The game took place at Hampden Park in Scotland, against Eintracht Frankfurt of West Germany (who'd routed Rangers, the Scots' own champions, 12–4 on aggregate in their semi-final).

Here's how to recreate the game in the playground:

●Pick a couple of teachers to play for you. One has to be a bit bald and 33 years old. Call him Alfredo di Stefano. He's got a really powerful left-footed shot, which he gives his dad the credit for by saying:

I was right-footed, so my father didn't let me play unless I would shoot the ball with my left foot.

●The other teacher also has to be 33 years old. He's not bald, but he is short and pudgy. Call him Ferenc Puskas.

● Once the game starts, don't do anything for 19 minutes. Then let the other team score.

● Now start to play. With you all playing your part, awesome Alfredo equalizes and then hits a second.

● Fabulous Ferenc has to join in now. He bangs in a goal before half time, then, after a nice cup of tea, another two in the second half to complete his hat-trick!

You're not finished yet. The game needs another four goals ... and keep an eye on your watch because they have to be scored in four minutes! Ferenc again, then the other team, then Alfredo to complete his own hat-trick, then a last goal for the other team.

●After 90 minutes, grab your calculators and work out what the score is! You should end up with

That amazing win was to see the end of their glorious run. The following year they were knocked out by deadly Spanish rivals Barcelona. But their five victories in a row has never been equalled. Here are five not-at-all-foul facts about those five fantastic seasons:

1 In their 37 European Cup games, Real scored 112 goals.

2 Reims' best player in the 1956 final was a Frenchman named Raymond Kopa – so Madrid bought him! He picked up winners' medals from then on.

3 It was a European Cup semi-final home leg on 11 April 1957 that saw Real Madrid's attendance record broken. The visitors (and losers) were Manchester United.

4 The 1960 final was the only one in which Hungarian hero Ferenc Puskas won a winner's medal for Real. He joined the club in 1958, but missed the 1959 final. His only other final appearance was in 1962, when Real were beaten 5–3 by the Portuguese team Benfica. It was some appearance, though: poacher Puskas scored all three Real goals.

5 Argentinain, Alfredo di Stefano – nicknamed "the white arrow" – scored in every one of Real Madrid's five winning finals.

The World Club Championship

In 1959, somebody had a bright idea. Why not have a trophy played for by the winners of the European Cup and the winners of the South American equivalent? There was only one problem with this bright idea: South America didn't have an equivalent competition.

This was easily solved. They invented one, called it the *Copa Libertadores,* and a year later Penarol of Uruguay were crowned South American champions. Everything was now ready for the big match to be played. And, as it was obviously going to be the biggest game between the biggest clubs of the two biggest football-playing continents, there seemed no point in calling it anything less than the World Club Cup.

208

Fittingly, Real Madrid became the first "world champions" in 1960 in Montevideo, winning the two-legged tie by whacking Penarol 5–1 in Madrid after drawing 0–0 in Montevideo. And, for the next few years, the annual match was a success. Between 1967 and 1971, though, something went horribly wrong. The matches became so violent that the competition should have been called The World Club-Each-Other-As-Much-As-Possible Cup.

The Kickin' World Club Championship Quiz

Here are some facts about the competition's history. Unfortunately, just like in many of the games, bits and pieces have flown everywhere. The underlined sections have ended up in the wrong sentences. Can you sort out the trouble?

1967 Celtic of Scotland meet Racing Club of Argentina.

a) As the teams come out for the start of the second-leg game, Celtic's goalkeeper Ronnie Simpson is <u>sent off in each leg</u>.

b) After both teams won a match each, there had to be a play-off game. In this game there were so many fights that at one point the players had to be <u>sent off</u>!

c) In this match <u>their opponents</u> were sent off!

d) Things got so confusing that one player finished the game even though he'd been <u>hit by a missile.</u>

209

1968 Manchester United play Estudiantes de la Plata of Argentina.

e) Estudiantes have already gained a reputation for dirty tricks in the *Copa Libertadores* – their players have even been known to stick pins in <u>five players</u>.

f) In two bad-tempered matches, United have a player <u>suspended on the orders of the President</u>.

1969 It's AC Milan's turn to face Estudiantes.

g) They manage to win 4–2 on aggregate, even though in Argentina their striker Nestor Combin <u>refused to take part</u>.

h) After the game, three Estudiantes players are <u>kept apart by armed police</u>.

1970 Estudiantes again, this time against Feyenoord of Holland. The Dutch side triumph in another dirty match.

i) Their winning goal is scored by Joop van Deale in spite of the fact that he <u>has his nose broken</u>.

j) 1971–1980 The competition goes into decline because nearly every European champion <u>has broken glasses</u>.

Answers:

a) As the teams come out, Celtic's goalkeeper Ronnie Simpson is hit by a missile. He had to be carried off and didn't play in the match.

b) At one point the players had to be kept apart by armed police. The ground looked more like a riot zone than a football pitch!

c) In this match five players were sent off! Two were from Racing Club and three from Celtic.

d) One player finished the game even though he'd been sent off! It was Celtic's Bertie Auld. After being sent off close to the end, he refused to leave the pitch. Rather than argue with him, the Paraguayan referee decided to finish the match.

e) Estudiantes players have even been known to stick pins in their opponents. Talk about giving the other side the needle!

f) United have a player sent off in each leg – Nobby Stiles in the away match and George Best at home. United lost 2–1 on aggregate.

g) AC Milan's striker Nestor Combin has his nose broken.

h) Three Estudiantes players are suspended on the orders of the President. Not only that, they're thrown into prison for a while.

i) Feyenoord's winning goal is scored by Joop van Deale in spite of the fact that he has broken glasses. Yes, he wore spectacles during matches and Estudiantes obviously thought it would be a good idea to bust them – only to learn that Joop found it no big Deale!

j) Virtually all the European champions refused to take part.

211

Yes, throughout the 1970s European Cup winners such as Ajax, Bayern Munich, Liverpool and Nottingham Forest all stayed at home rather than risk the foulest of games. The cup was about to die. Then, dashing to the rescue, came a saviour from – where?

Answer: c) Deciding that it would be a good way of bringing top-class football to Japan (and getting their company name widely advertised, of course) Japanese car manufacturer Toyota saved the World Club Cup in 1980 by becoming its sponsor. They lay down just one important condition: the match must always be played in Japan! It was, very successfully, for 25 years. Then, in 2005, it was replaced by the FIFA Club World Championship. This is contested annually by the 6 champion clubs from FIFA's world regions. In 2008 it was won by Manchester United!

THE DON'T TRY TO FOUL ME IN A BIG GAME AWARD...

Jose Aguas (Benfica). Sharp-shooting Jose played for Portuguese champions Benfica when they became the first club to beat Real Madrid and win the European Cup. Legend has it that before leaving his country, Angola, to become a professional footballer, he had been a lion-hunter!

REFS RULE, OK!

Who'd be the poor referee having to cope with the sort of foul behaviour the World Club Cup produced? In fact, who'd be a referee? The man in the middle is given no end of trouble the world over.

That wasn't always the way. When organized football began using the English rules, referees weren't in the middle of the pitch at all. They would be at the side of the pitch, looking on, rather like a cricket umpire. They worked in a similar way to cricket umpires, too. If a player thought a foul had been committed or a goal scored, he would appeal. The referee would then either stop the game or, if he disagreed with the appeal, tell the teams to play on.

The people who understood the English rules best, of course, were the English. It's no surprise, then, that the best-known referee from those early days was an Englishman...

The royal ref

Referees are usually called foul names, so the first unusual fact about John Lewis is that he was actually given a nice name because he was so fair. They called him *The Prince of Referees*. He started off as a player with Blackburn Rovers, a club he also helped to found, only  becoming a referee after a skating accident forced him to give up playing. Nobody ever questioned John's judgement by accusing him of being a cheat. Lewis was as upright as they came. He didn't smoke, drink or gamble – and he donated all his refereeing fees to charity! Lewis refereed three FA Cup Finals (1895, 1896, 1897). Although he "retired" in 1905, he was often invited to get his whistle out again. He was still blowing it fifteen years later, in 1920, when he refereed the Olympic Games football final between Belgium and Spain – at the age of 65!

No-nonsense Howcroft

Jack "Jimmy" Howcroft looked more like a bank manager than an international-class referee. When he walked out to referee the 1920 FA Cup Final between Aston Villa and Huddersfield Town he was wearing shorts to his knees, a white shirt, a bow tie and a smart black jacket with a white handkerchief  in the top pocket!

He stood for no nonsense, though, and the players knew it. Villa's captain that day was a hard man named

Frank Barson. Howcroft gave him an early warning, saying: "The first wrong move you make, Barson, off you go." How early? In the changing rooms before the game began! It worked, too. Barson was as good as gold and Howcroft had an easy game.

Dan, Dan the karate man

One of the best-known English referees in the modern game is Uriah Rennie. Players don't mess with him either, because as a kickboxing instructor and karate black belt 1st dan, rock-hard Rennie is tougher and fitter than they are! He's also a magistrate in his home town of Sheffield, so he knows a bit about dishing out a punishment to fit the crime. He  doesn't care what the fans shout, either. He once said, "To go to Old Trafford or Highbury and referee games is not pressure. That's an honour."

The ball juggler

So did refereeing skills travel overseas in the same way as playing skills? Of course. The referee for the first-ever World Cup final in 1930 was a Belgian, John Langenus. He had to make a big decision before a ball was even kicked – whose ball were they going to play with? Uruguay and Argentina had reached the final and both

215

wanted to play the match with a ball made in their own country. So how did Juggler John resolve the problem? By playing one half of the match with each ball!

That was an easy decision compared to one Langenus had been asked to make while attempting to qualify as a referee. The examination paper asked him to imagine what he would do if he was in charge of a game during which the ball was kicked high in the air and landed in the cockpit of a passing aeroplane. Langenus didn't know – and failed the exam! He told this story years later in his autobiography. At that time the most famous referee in the world, John Langenus couldn't resist adding that in all the games he'd refereed he'd never once had the ball stolen by a thieving pilot.

A shining example

Until he retired in 2005, most agreed that Italian referee Pierluigi Collina was the best in the world. Players were taking a big risk if they swore at Pierluigi, because the chances were he'd understand them. Apart from Italian, he spoke English, Spanish and French! At a gangly 1.88m tall, with a shining bald head and bulging blue eyes,  Collina's become more famous than a lot of the players he controlled. There are websites about him (including his own official site, from which you can even download his autograph!), and in 2003 peerless Pierluigi published his autobiography called *The Rules of the Game.*

The woman in the middle

Commentators have often called the referee "the man in the middle". Soon they may have to get used to referring to the woman in the middle. On 14 August 2003 Nicole Petignat made history by becoming the first woman to referee a UEFA men's competition match, when she took charge of the UEFA Cup qualifying first-leg match between AIK Solna of Sweden and Fylkir of Iceland.

CRYING WON'T HELP...

Referees and Ruffians

Foul Fans

Referees expect to get shouted at by the crowd. After all, they can't win. Any decision they make in favour of one team is a decision against the other team. Some things they get from spectators are even fouler, though...

- In 1996 a match between Uruguayan sides Penarol and Danubio was abandoned after the crowd began throwing things at the officials. The referee ignored the stones and coins but refused to carry on after one of his linesmen was knocked out by a crash helmet!

- English referee Paul Durkin had a nasty fright during a match at Oldham in 1999. Looking down at his shirt, he saw it covered in what looked like blood. To his great relief he quickly realized it wasn't. It was tomato ketchup. He'd been hit by a hot dog!

- But perhaps the most unexpected thing aimed at a referee came from a man named Sye Webster, a fan of Scottish club Arbroath. So happy was Sye that his team had just rattled in five goals in their league match against East Stirling, that he raced on to the pitch and gave the referee a big kiss. Was it appreciated? By the referee, perhaps, but not by anybody else. Sad Sye was banned from the ground for a year for invading the pitch!

Fouler Footballers

Ricky Rubbish can make as many mistakes as he likes, but just let him spot a referee slipping up and he'll be giving him a hard time. Some players don't stop at talking, though...

- Maybe because he'd heard about referee Pierluigi Collina's command of languages, AC Milan defender Jose Chamot didn't say a word at the end of their match against Juventus in 1998. He simply marched up, shook Collina's hand ... and earned himself a one-match ban for dissent. Why? Milan had lost 1–0 and Chamot, none too pleased, had done his best to crush the ref's fingers!

- At least Chamot could argue that he was being over-friendly. Goalkeeper James Nanoor, playing in a 1999 African Champions League match, had no defence when he spat in the face of referee Zinco Zeli. He received a one-year ban.

- It happens at all levels of the game. Somerset Sunday-league player Lee Todd was sent off for using foul and abusive language after just two seconds of a match in 2000. Why? He claimed the referee had blown the whistle too close to his ear!

- Some players don't know when to stop being foul. In a 2006 World Cup game against Australia, Croatian Josip Simunic earned a yellow card from referee Graham Poll ... then another. But when Poll failed to send him off, what did silly Simunic do? Commit another foul! This time he did get sent off.

- He should have thanked his lucky stars he wasn't

Luigi Coluccio, suspended for nine days after being sent off in an Italian local league match. Coluccio didn't serve the ban – but only because he was shot dead in a mafia-linked gun battle not long after.

THE YOU'RE-STILL-BANNED-EVEN-THOUGH-YOU'RE DEAD AWARD...

Luigi Coluccio who still had his ban added to his club's record even though he wasn't alive to serve it. The league organizers said it could influence which team won the league's fair play award that season!

● Maybe referees should take a tip from English referee Peter Rhodes. He had no trouble from the Los Angeles Toros and Atlanta Braves teams when he was in charge of their match in the USA league in 1978. Maybe that was because both teams knew he had a gun in his pocket! It was there because one of the odd league rules required him to fire shots two minutes before the end of each half to let everybody know how the time was going.

YOU'RE SUPPOSED TO FIRE IT IN THE AIR!

Diabolically difficult decisions

Whether or not fans and players like their decisions, it's a referee's job to make them. Not simply during the game, either. Their first job is to decide whether to start a match at all. Then, once the game has started, they have to decide when to finish it! Sounds easy? Get your whistle out, then, and have a go at making some diabolically difficult decisions!

Let's start in England (where else?)...

1 It's 1888 and you're in charge of a big FA cup fifth round tie between Aston Villa and Preston North End. After the crowd invade the pitch for the fourth time, Preston complain that they can't be expected to play an important cup match like this. **Continue or abandon?**

2 You're in charge of another FA cup first round tie, this time between Grimsby Town and Southern League side Croydon Common in 1911. The Croydon players have been slipping over on the pitch and at half-time they spend over 20 minutes putting new studs in their boots. **Continue or abandon?**

3 It's Easter Monday, 1915, and you're Mr H Smith, refereeing Oldham Athletic v Middlesbrough in the old First Division (now the Premiership). In the second half you decide to send off Oldham's Billy Cook after he commits a couple of bad fouls. He refuses to go. You pull out your watch and give him one minute to get off. A minute later he's still there. **Continue or abandon?**

Now to discover whether you're a world-class decision-maker...

4 It's 1906 and you're about to start an international match when the Lord Mayor of London strolls on to the pitch arm-in-arm with a French film starlet and the President of the United States. The Lord Mayor insists that his guests both use one foot each to take the kick-off. **Start or don't start?**

5 It's 1949 and it's getting really dark – so dark that the players in the match you're refereeing are having trouble seeing the brown leather ball. You're about to abandon the game when suddenly a white ball is produced. **Continue or abandon?**

6 You're in charge of the Scotland v Austria match on 8 May 1963 at Hampden Park. It's supposed to be a friendly, but you've already sent off one Austrian for spitting, and another for a waist-high tackle. There are still 11 minutes to go. **Continue or abandon?**

7 It's 11 July 1966 and you're Hungarian referee Istvan Szolt. It's a big day. You're to be in charge of the World Cup Group 1 match between England and Uruguay at Wembley. However, the rules say that the players of both teams are supposed to show you their special identity cards but seven of England's well-known stars have left theirs behind. **Start or don't start?**

8 It's 1994 and you're about to referee a big international match between Portugal and Germany. You speak Portuguese and German, but no English. **Start or don't start?**

222

Answers:

1 Continue ... but you announce that the match won't count as a cup-tie, only a friendly. (Referees were *really* powerful in 1888!) After they'd won the game 3–1, though, Preston changed their minds. They wanted the result to count as a cup win. Villa argued back that

SOME FRIENDLY!

they'd played most of the game as a friendly! In the ensuing row, the FA came down on Preston's side. Why? Because, they said, Villa were responsible for the fans who'd caused all the trouble!

2 Continue ... but it should have been Abandon. The FA say that a half-time interval can't last longer than 20 minutes and order the game to be replayed – even though innocent Grimsby won the match 3–0. They make Croydon pay for it in the replay. This time they win 8–1!

3 Abandon. Mr Smith marched off the field and took the two teams with him. Oldham were fined £350 (worth about £16,500 today) and Cook was suspended for a year.

4 Start. It wasn't until 1907 that a rule was introduced saying that an official match had to be kicked-off by one of the players involved!

5 Abandon. You don't have any choice. The rules didn't allow games to be played with a white ball until 1950!

THE SUPER SAVER'S AWARD...

Liverpool FC who, according to goalie Tommy Lawrence (their super saver of the 1950s), wouldn't fork out for an expensive white ball but slopped white paint onto a normal one. If bits came off during a match they'd just dab some more on before the next game!

QUICK-DRYING PAINT'S EXPENSIVE AS WELL!

6 Abandon. Both sides had been at it and the referee, Jim Finney, said afterwards, "I felt that I had to abandon the match or somebody would have been seriously hurt."

7 Start. But only after Szolt made England trainer Harold Shepherdson race back to the team hotel to get the identity cards!

8 Don't start. In fact, you should really send yourself off! In 1992 the world football governing body FIFA ruled that all international referees had to be able to speak English.

YOU KNOW THE RULES. NOW OFF YOU GO!

Red Card Rumpuses

Spotting infringements is another part of the tough job a referee has. "Was that tackle a foul?" he has to ask. If so, was it a foul worth a yellow card? Or was it an even fouler foul worthy of a red card?

At least with coloured cards to wave the player concerned won't be in any doubt about what the referee's decided. And where did the idea of red and yellow cards come from? You've guessed it – England!

The man who gave them the green light was ex-referee Ken Aston. When the 1966 World Cup was held in England he'd retired from the middle and was in charge of the team of referees. He was forced to step forward, though, when the Argentina v England game turned out to be the foulest match of the whole tournament. German referee Rudolf Kreitlein tried to send off Argentina's non-German-speaking captain Antonio Rattin – who refused to leave the pitch until Aston, using his schoolboy Spanish, finally made him understand.

Driving home afterwards, Aston was still thinking of how referees could leave players in no doubt about what they'd decided when he was stopped by a red traffic light ... which then switched to yellow ... and promptly turned on a light in Aston's head! Red and yellow cards were on the way in.

So, red and yellow cards help a referee make his decisions clear. But, as these international stories show, that isn't always the end of the matter...

Hot meal

Referees always take a spare watch and pencil onto the pitch with them. They don't expect to need a spare red card – but when the referee in charge of the 1989 Italian league match between Pianta and Arpax showed his to Pianta's Fernando d'Ercoli, it was the last he saw of it. Furious Fernando snatched the card from his hand – and ate it!

CAN I HAVE THE YELLOW FOR AFTERS?

Diving exhibition

An equally foul, if not even fouler Italian, was Paulo Di Canio. After referee Paul Alcock sent him off while playing for Sheffield Wednesday against Arsenal in 1998, demented Di Canio shoved Alcock in the chest. To

226

make matters even worse he accused the referee of diving! "It was just a slight push," said potty Paulo, "and he took two or three paces back and fell over!" The English FA weren't convinced. They banned Di Canio for 11 matches and fined him £10,000.

Take that!

Unlike Alcock, Chilean first-division referee Francisco Camaano wasn't prepared to take things lying down. During an argument that took place in the last minute of a match between Deportes Temuco and Audax Italiano in July 2002, Audax's Alejandro Carrasco made the mistake of stamping on Camaano's foot. The referee didn't hesitate. Instead of wasting time fishing for his red card, cruncher Camaano promptly kneed the offending player between the legs! "It was self-defence!" he claimed, as agonized Alejandro rolled around the pitch. Camaano realized he'd done wrong, though. After the game he announced his retirement from refereeing – much to the relief of players everywhere!

I cannot tell a lie

Another official who wasn't too proud to admit he'd made a mistake was English referee Stephen Lodge, in 1993. After realising he'd sent off the wrong player during a league match between Oxford United and Sunderland, solemn Stephen knew what he had to do. The next day he wrote to the Football Association – and reported himself!

Flag-unhappy

Amateur matches can produce just as many red-card rumpuses for referees. When Peppermill met the Gardeners Arms in the Blackpool Sunday Alliance League in 1996, a touchline collision between Gardeners Arms striker Tim Yeo and a linesman ended up with the referee giving a red card to ... the linesman! A Peppermill supporter doing the job as a volunteer, he'd taken offence at being flattened and hit Yeo over the head with his flag!

The nutty nettings game

But perhaps the trickiest call for a referee is that of deciding when a goal has been scored. Usually it's easy. The net bulges, the goalkeeper buries his head in his hands before getting up to blame his defenders (who are all holding their heads in their hands and/or blaming the goalkeeper) and all is clear-cut. But sometimes ... well look at the next two pages and see for yourself by having a go at this goal-grabbing game.

For each question simply decide 'goal' or 'no goal'. Will you hit the back of the net or hammer the ball over the bar? Time to put on your shooting boots!

1. WEDNESDAY (THE CLUB OFFICIALLY CHANGED THEIR NAME TO SHEFFIELD WEDNESDAY IN 1929 BUT PRIOR TO THIS THEY WERE KNOWN AS THE WEDNESDAY) V BOLTON, 1885. WHEN WEDNESDAY GET THE BALL IN THE NET THE REFEREE CHEERS. GOAL OR NO GOAL?

2. BADALONA V TARRAGONA, SPANISH CUP, 1983. REBOLLO OF BADALONA RUNS IN TO TAKE A PENALTY - AFTER WHICH SANTIAGO OF TARRAGONA GIVES HIM A HUG. GOAL OR NO GOAL?

3. BARNSLEY V MANCHESTER UNITED, FA CUP FOURTH ROUND, 1938. FRANK BOKAS OF BARNSLEY TAKES A THROW-IN. UNITED'S GOALKEEPER TOM BREEN JUST TOUCHES THE BALL BUT IT GOES OVER HIS HEAD AND INTO THE UNITED NET. GOAL OR NO GOAL?

4. TOTTENHAM HOTSPUR V HUDDERSFIELD TOWN, THE OLD FIRST DIVISION, 1951-52 SEASON. EDDIE BAILY OF TOTTENHAM TAKES A CORNER AND HITS THE REFEREE ON THE BACK MAKING HIM FALL FLAT ON HIS FACE! THE BALL REBOUNDS TO BAILY WHO CENTRES FOR STRIKER LEN DUQUEMIN TO SCORE. GOAL OR NO GOAL?

⑤ CELTIC V FALKIRK, SCOTTISH DIVISION 'A',
1953. CELTIC'S CHARLIE TULLY SCORES
DIRECT FROM A CORNER - BUT WHILE HE WAS
TAKING THE KICK THERE WERE SOME
SPECTATORS ON THE PITCH.
GOAL OR NO GOAL?

⑥ TAGHMON V TOMBRUCK UNITED, IRISH
WEXFORD LEAGUE. TAGHMON'S GOALIE SHANE
KEHOE SWOOPS TO MAKE A SAVE. AS HE DOES
SO, HIS BASEBALL CAP FALLS OFF. KEHOE
STEPS BACK, PICKS IT UP, THEN BOOTS THE
BALL UPFIELD. GOAL OR NO GOAL?

⑦ ECUADOR V VENEZUELA, 1996 OLYMPIC
GAMES QUALIFYING MATCH. AS ECUADOR'S
DEFENDER MATAMBA TAKES A PENALTY HIS
BOOT COMES OFF. BOOT AND BALL BOTH SAIL
INTO THE VENEZUELA NET.
GOAL OR NO GOAL?

⑧ EARL'S COLNE RESERVES V WIMPOLE
2000, ESSEX LEAGUE, 2002. THE REFEREE'S
FOOT COMES INTO CONTACT WITH THE BALL
AND IT GOES INTO THE EARL'S COLNE NET.
GOAL OR NO GOAL?

⑨ BOLTON WANDERERS V EVERTON, FA CARLING
PREMIERSHIP, 1997. BOLTON'S GERRY TAGGART
FIRES IN A HEADER WHICH LOOKS TO HAVE CROSSED
THE LINE. THE BOLTON TEAM SHOUT "GOAL";
EVERTON'S SHOUT "NO GOAL". THE LINESMAN
THINKS "NO GOAL" TOO. WHAT DOES THE REFEREE
DECIDE? GOAL OR NO GOAL?

Answers:

1 Goal. Wednesday were amateurs, Bolton professionals. As being paid for playing football was frowned on in 1885, referees often favoured the amateurs!

2 No goal, twice over. Tarragona hugged Rebello because he'd missed the penalty. The referee booked him for ungentlemanly conduct and ordered the kick to be taken again. Rebello did – and missed again.

GREAT PENALTY!

3 Goal. If the United 'keeper hadn't touched the ball it wouldn't have counted, but as he did it went down as an own goal.

4 No goal. A referee doesn't count as a player, so Baily can't touch the ball again until some other player has. Unfortunately, with his nose in the mud, the referee assumed that's what had happened – so he gave the goal and Tottenham won the match 1–0!

5 No goal. Correctly, the referee disallowed it. So Tully just shrugged, took the corner again – and scored again!

6 Goal. Correctly, the referee gave a goal. After the goalie's cap had fallen off, the wind had blown it over his goal line and into the net. Shtupid Shane had still been holding the ball when he went to collect it!

7 Goal – but the referee wrongly said "No goal" and ordered the kick to be retaken. He then made another mistake as Matamba's boot flew off again, this time hitting a post while the ball hit the crossbar. Instead of ordering yet another kick, the referee waved play on – and Ecuador lost the match 5–2.

8 Goal. Wimpole were losing 18–1 ... so, feeling sorry for them, referee Brian Savill deliberately scored to make it 18–2! Taking a dim view of this generosity, the FA banned him for seven weeks. Wimpole were happy, though – Savill's goal had made the referee their joint top scorer!

9 Goal. That's what the all-seeing TV cameras later proved. Unfortunately, referee Stephen Lodge had said "No goal" causing Bolton to draw 0–0 instead of winning 1–0. Did it matter? Yes. At the end of the season Bolton were relegated on inferior goal difference – to Everton!

THE AIR-TODAY-GONE-TOMORROW AWARD...

Every Referee. According to the rules of football, if the ball hits the referee it's as if it hasn't happened. The referee has to be treated as "air"!

PUFF!

Gone Away

What with all the foul pressures and even fouler abuse they face, it's a wonder that referees turn up to do their job at all. So let's end this chapter with a couple of examples of times when they really haven't turned up.

Liverpool were playing Huddersfield Town at Anfield in the old First Division in 1948. The first half had finished and everybody had trooped off for the break. Then...

The whistle had been blown by somebody in the crowd.

233

On that occasion it was an accident that the referee wasn't around. Sometimes they really do go slow on purpose.

- In December 1998, Albanian referees deliberately started matches 15 minutes late in protest at the abuse they were getting.
- The Halifax Referee's Society in West Yorkshire had gone even further in 1995. They'd held a strike, causing 50 matches to be called off!

So why do referees do it? Because, foul as it can be, they love the game. And, let's face it, football would be even fouler without them!

 THE DEVOTION TO YOUR HUSBAND EVEN THOUGH EVERYBODY ELSE WOULD LIKE TO WRING HIS NECK AWARD...

Mrs Stephen Lodge, referee's wife. When asked in an interview why he does the job, English referee Stephen Lodge said:

I enjoy it – and my wife's very keen. She's my number one supporter. She's probably my only supporter!

CRAFTY COACHING

Players have to play (foul or otherwise), but it's the manager/coach whose job it is to tell them how to play.

NO, YOU CAN PLAY SNAKES AND LADDERS AFTER YOU'VE BEATEN MANCHESTER UNITED.

So, where did the idea of football tactics come from? England, along with plenty of other ideas? The answer to that is ... not likely!

In England, the man in charge of the team was called a "manager". That's because he managed things, like buying and selling players and arguing about how much (or how little to pay them). The idea of a manager telling players how to play was seen as very odd – even by the managers themselves. England's first-ever international manager, Walter Winterbottom, wasn't appointed until 1946 (74 years after England's first game!). Even then, he didn't talk about tactics. In those days wall-to-wall TV coverage wasn't around, so Walter would concentrate on telling the players about their opponents – because he was the only one who'd seen them play!

Top tactics were far more advanced outside England. There, the man in charge of the team was called a "coach" – because his main job was seen as coaching the players. And the best coaches didn't simply devise tactics that suited their players; they devised tactics that nobody had ever thought of before. That way the opposing coaches didn't have the tactics to tackle their tactics, if you get the idea. No? Here are some world-famous examples.

Helenio's hell

Helenio Herrera was coach at Internazionale of Milan (known as Inter) in the 1960s. His terrible tactics were based on the theory that if you don't let a goal in then you only need to score one to win – and even if you don't manage that, you still won't lose! In other words, Inter concentrated on defence. Here's how to do it with your school team:

- Pick four defenders who like making friends.
- When the match starts, get each of these defenders to be so friendly towards one of the other team's forwards that they follow them everywhere. This is called man-to-man marking.

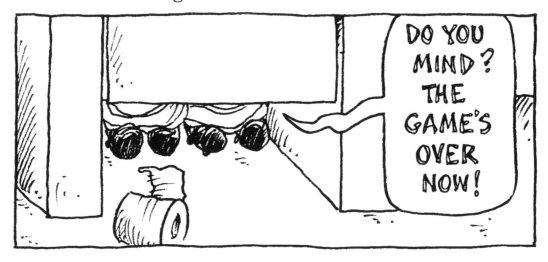

- Choose another defender who wants to be a cleaner when s/he grows up.
- Call this defender a "sweeper". His/her job is to patrol behind the four friendly defenders and be ready to run

over and deal with any attacker who manages to get away from his friendly defender.

- Finally, find a goalkeeper with a large supply of warm underwear. With this tactic s/he won't have anything to do, and might get chilly with all the standing about.

Helenio's hellish system was known as *catenaccio* – the door bolt – because it was so effective at shutting out opposing forwards. Unfortunately, it was so boring that it made fans bolt for the door!

Rinus's runabouts

If you think *catenaccio* sounds chronic then read on! Rinus Michels did too. He was the coach of Dutch team Ajax between 1965 and 1971 who, more than anyone, came up with the way to cope with defensive opponents. Here's the way to do it with your team:

- Pick ten out-field players who can't decide whether they want to be forwards, midfield men or defenders.
- Throw the team's shirts on the floor and say, "Wear any one you like. The number on the back doesn't matter!"
- Before the game starts, have the team line up roughly the way you'd expect ... with number 2 nearer to

your goalkeeper than number 9.

● But all that changes once the game begins!

● If number 2 sees an attacking chance down the left wing, s/he can go for it!

● If number 9 spots danger, s/he can rush back to help out.

● In fact, just so as long as there are always the right number of bodies in defence, midfield and attack, the players can run anywhere and everywhere!

Rinus's runabout system was called *the whirl* because the Ajax players were allowed to whirl from one position to another. This made it impossible for the man-to-man marking system of *catenaccio* to operate, of course, because the opposing defenders didn't know whom they were supposed to make friends with.

The whirl needed talented players who were good enough to play in any position, but that's just what Ajax had. Between 1971 and 1973 they were European Champions three years in succession, with the second being the most satisfying victory of all. They ran out 2–0 winners ... against Internazionale!

Stupid Scolari's scumbags

Don't get the idea that every continental coach was crafty and calculating. Luis Felipe Scolari, manager of Brazilian side Palmeiras in the 1990s, prided himself on being foul – and liked his players to be even fouler!

When asked in 1999 about some of the tough tackles his team were making he replied:

Nobody can afford to lose now, so I ask my players to commit more fouls in midfield.

Was Luis a lone leader in the fouling field? Not according to him:

The other coaches say they don't tell their players to do this. But the fact is that I'm stupid because I tell the truth while others lie.

Partick's partners

Foul Felipe he may have been, but Scolari's methods worked. He won 9 trophies in Brazil, before leading the country to triumph in the 2002 World Cup. After that, he became coach of Portugal, taking them to the final of Euro 2004 and the quarter-finals of Euro 2008, also fourth place in World Cup 2006. In July 2008, Scolari became coach of Chelsea. Opposing teams should watch out for choppier Chelsea challenges!

Every coach tries to make substitutions when things aren't going well. Their aim is always to take off a tired player and put on a fresh one, or take off an out-of-form player and put on one they hope will whack in a five-minute hat trick.

So the leaders in imaginative substitutions simply have to be Bertie Auld and Pat Quinn, joint managers of Scots club Partick Thistle. On one occasion – and even though they'd already used all their substitutes – the prickly Thistle management men decided that Partick player Jim Melrose was performing so badly they'd take him off and make do with 10 men. It worked, too. Thistle bloomed and won the match 2–1!

Money Managers

Club managers in England might not have led the way in tactical talking but they knew their stuff off the pitch.

Herbert Chapman, manager of Huddersfield Town and Arsenal in the 1920s and 1930s, was one of the clearest thinkers in the game. He foresaw many of the football features we now take for granted, such as floodlit matches, live commentaries and even numbers on football shirts. He knew plenty about the value of publicity, too. Chapman persuaded London Transport to change the name of the station closest to Highbury (where Arsenal played between 1913-2005) from the boring *Gillespie Road* to – you've guessed it – Arsenal. Free advertising on every single map of the underground!

Chapman knew the value of a clear head when it came to transfer deals, too. In 1928 he desperately wanted to buy England international David Jack from

Bolton Wanderers and was willing to smash the transfer record of £6,500 to get him; if necessary even to pay over £10,000! (Don't laugh. Even though in today's money £10,000 is worth "only" £500,000, no football club had ever paid as much for a player).

So off Chapman went, with his assistant, to meet the Bolton officials at the Euston Hotel in London. They arrived early...

So Herbert Chapman got his man. David Jack scored 25 goals in the remaining 31 matches of that season and Arsenal's all-conquering team of the 1930s were on their way.

Sadly, Chapman wasn't quite so good at managing his own health. After catching a chill in January 1934, his doctor told him to stay indoors. Instead, he went off in the freezing cold to watch Arsenal's third team play, saying, "I haven't seen the boys for a week or so." He never saw them again after that. His chill turned to pneumonia and he died three days later.

Crafty Coaching's Testing Ten Quiz

Nowadays coaches (and managers) don't stay at home any more – wherever it is. Football is a world game and coaches travel the world.

At the 2006 World Cup, for instance, Saudi Arabia's coach was Brazilian, so was Portugal's and so was Japan's. Togo's coach came from Germany and Australia had a Dutchman in charge. Even England didn't have an Englishman leading them – their coach, Sven Goran Erikkson, came from Sweden!

So, what does it take to be a top coach? Where have the most corking coaches come from? Is this one area in which fabulous foreigners have led the field or have there been some excellent Englishmen?

Come to some decisions by making some decisions about the testing ten questions in this quiz! We'll begin with three about Englishmen:

1 Bill Lambton was a typically rugged English coach. After training English boxers in Denmark he took over at Leeds United in 1957. During one of his first coaching sessions he told the players they should be able to – what?

KICK A FOOTBALL IN BARE FEET AND NOT FEEL IT.

IMPROVE THEIR HAND-EYE COORDINATION BY TRYING TO PUNCH EACH OTHER.

STAY SUPPLE BY BOUNCING ON A TRAMPOLINE.

2 A top coach has to have confidence in his own ability. Brian Clough was a double championship winner, first in charge of Derby County, then Nottingham Forest (who also won the European Cup twice). When asked whether he thought he'd been a good manager, Clough said: "I wouldn't say I was the best manager in the business. But I was in the top..." – what?

3 A conscientious coach will support his players through thick and thicker – like Aston Villa's Graham Taylor in 2002. Explaining that his England international striker Darius Vassell wasn't going to be fit for a match because of a self-inflicted injury he added kindly, "He was only trying to be helpful." What had Darius done?

CUT A HAND WASHING HIS VILLA SHIRT

FELL OFF A LADDER TRYING TO MOVE A TV AERIAL TO GET A BETTER PICTURE

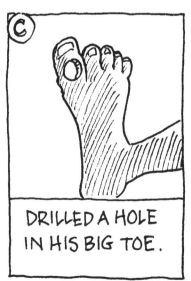

DRILLED A HOLE IN HIS BIG TOE.

Time to move abroad now – but only as far as Scotland for three questions about Scots coaches:

4 Coaches have to show understanding if their players get injured during a match. When Partick Thistle's John Labie was told in 1993 that his striker Colin McGlashan had sustained a head injury and didn't know who he was, Labie's immediate response was, "Tell him he's..." – what?

a) Scottish.

b) Playing for us.

c) Pele.

5 A top coach will do everything to make his players comfortable. When Liverpool arrived at their hotel the evening before their European Cup semi-final against Internazionale in 1965, their Scots manager Bill Shankly was disturbed to discover that every fifteen minutes bells would chime out loudly from a nearby monastery. What did he do to try and help his lads get a good night's sleep?

a) ISSUE EVERY PLAYER WITH A SET OF LIVERPOOL EARPLUGS.

b) ASK MONKS AT THE MONASTERY TO MUFFLE THEIR BELLS.

C) PLAY LOUD MUSIC TO DROWN OUT THE CHIMES.

6 A coach must convince everybody that he knows where his team is headed. Scots manager Tommy Docherty knew exactly what to say to get the job with Rotherham United in 1967: "Chairman, I promise to take this club out of the Second Division." Did Docherty do it?

a) Yes.

b) No.

Now three coaches who travelled to England to show the birthplace of football how to do it:

7 A top coach knows how to keep everybody happy – including himself. In 2002 Claudio Ranieri, an Italian in charge of Chelsea, said: "I am happy when our fans are happy, when our players are happy and our chairman is..." – what?

HAPPY AS A PARROT

ON THE MOON

SMILING FROM EAR TO THERE

8 A top coach doesn't let language difficulties get in the way. Frenchman Arsène Wenger faced a problem at his new club Arsenal in 1998 when his fellow countryman, striker Nicolas Anelka, told him he thought Dutch winger Marc Overmars was a load of rubbish. What did multi-lingual Wenger do?

a) Agree with Anelka.

b) Tell Overmars what Anelka had said.

c) Arrange a fight between them.

9 Not only multi-lingual, but multi-talented, Arsène Wenger showed that a top coach also has to master the art of dealing with his team's disciplinary problems. After Arsenal had finished the season with a total of nine red cards, wily Wenger said – what?

a) "We probably deserved half of them."

b) "Next season we will get less than ten."

c) "Did we? I lost count."

And, finally, a question which applies to coaches the whole world over:

10 A top coach believes in his team, come what may. After watching his Dutch league team, AZ Alkmaar, lose 5–1 at home to Roda JC in 2003, coach Co Adriaanse turned up at the post-match press conference and said of the result: "This does not mean..." – what?

Answers:

1a) Future England defender Jack Charlton promptly asked Lambton to show them how ... and the coach ended up hobbling from the training pitch. A great believer in the benefits of trampolining, he got players doing **c)** as well!

2a) Clough wasn't known for his modesty.

3c) In an attempt to burst a painful blood blister, dozy Darius had drilled a hole in his toenail with a DIY electric drill! All he did was cause an infection and ended up having half his nail removed. Oh yes ... and he had to put up with the  newspapers calling him the Aston Drilla!

4c) Making it the one and only time that the famous Brazilian turned out for Partick Thistle!

5b) Either they couldn't or wouldn't. Perhaps the monks were Inter fans!

6a) Unfortunately, Docherty took them in the wrong direction. Rotherham were relegated and went down to the old Third Division (now League One)!

7b) What Ranieri had still to discover was that the football-speak phrase he wanted was "over the moon". Or perhaps he thought that his team still had further to go!

8b) ... kind of. Both players were with him at the time, but Anelka only spoke French and Overmars didn't. So Wenger told his winger that Anelka had just said what a good player he was – and watched, beaming, as the two shook hands!

9a) Half of nine is four-and-a-half, of course. Wenger

didn't manage to explain what punishment half a red card would deserve!

IT MEANS I'M SENDING YOU OFF BUT YOU CAN COME BACK ON AGAIN.

10c) Adriaanse then added, "That is scoreboard journalism." Strangely enough, the newspapers next day, still reported that AZ Alkmaar had lost 5–1!

What does the future hold for coaches? If developments in Italy are any clue, there's a chance it could get fairer rather than fouler. In 2003, Luciano Gaucci, President of league club AC Perugia, made it quite clear that he expected to be signing women players for his club one day – and listed the reasons why:

Women are more intelligent than men in general. They are more methodical and precise. I have seen girls playing much better than men. We have signed teenagers and they became great players. We can do the same things with girls!

GLOBAL GROUNDS AND DEADLY DERBIES

Nowadays the mere mention of the words "football ground" conjures up a picture of a lush green pitch surrounded by towering grandstands full of seats that cost oodles of money to sit in. But in football's early days things were very different. Pitches were just open fields, the conditions for the players were pretty foul – and any spectator who sat down risked landing on something even fouler!

THEY'RE GOING TO REGRET THROWING US OUT OF OUR FIELD!

Grounds became grander as football became more popular. Terraces were built to give fans a better view, covered areas kept the rain off, and proper seats meant the game could be watched in comfort.

As time went by, some of these football grounds became famous in their own right. They'd be remembered for the star players who'd played on their pitches and the magnificent matches they'd staged. And, sometimes, the grounds would become well known for things that had nothing at all to do with football. . .

The Wembley or Highbury quiz

Two of the most famous grounds in England were Wembley Stadium, home of the England team, and Highbury Stadium, home of Premiership team Arsenal. ("Were", because they've both been knocked down! Arsenal left Highbury for the Emirates Stadium in 2006 and England have been playing at 'new' Wembley since 2007.) Which ground goes with each of the following facts?

1 It was built on the remains of a college for training clergymen. **Highbury or Wembley?**

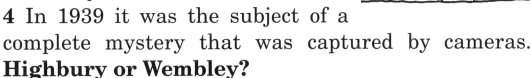

2 It was often entered by runaway dogs. **Highbury or Wembley?**

3 Its grass was specially grown – for playing golf! **Highbury or Wembley?**

4 In 1939 it was the subject of a complete mystery that was captured by cameras. **Highbury or Wembley?**

5 1951 saw a pair of eerily luminous green things land behind each of its goals. **Highbury or Wembley?**

6 An opponent once described its pitch as looking like "a comfortable bed you could lie down and sleep on". **Highbury or Wembley?**

7 There was no sleeping on duty there during World War Two! **Highbury or Wembley?**

8 It saw international boots for the first time in 1924, not to mention plenty of tricks from men who knew the ropes! **Highbury or Wembley?**

9 During the 1970s and 1980s Liverpool appeared there

so often their fans began to call it "Anfield South"!

Highbury or Wembley?

10 It's said to be haunted by a manager's ghost.

Highbury or Wembley?

Answers:

1 Highbury. Maybe that's why the prayers of the Arsenal fans that the score will stay at 1–0 to them, have so often been answered!

2 Wembley. From 1927 until the stadium closed in 2000, Wembley staged greyhound racing every Saturday night. Getting the stadium ready meant moving 20,000 seats to make way for the track. Such was the panic that on Cup Final day both sets of goalposts would have been removed even before the spectators had left the ground.

3 Wembley. The famously lush Wembley turf was grown at Ganton Golf Club in North Yorkshire. Once it had been laid, the Wembley ground staff would do anything to keep it looking at its best. On the morning of the Cup Final they'd all get down on their knees and weed it with dining forks!

4 Highbury. A black-and-white feature film was shot there, called *The Arsenal Stadium Mystery*. It was about a footballer who was poisoned during a match!

5 Highbury. The luminous green things were sightscreens, designed to make the white goals stand out more clearly. They were brought out if one of the dense London fogs of the 1950s was threatening to cause a match to be called off.

6 Wembley. The player was Sedun Odegbame of Nigeria, talking about the world-famous turf before his country met England in 1994.

7 Highbury. The stadium was used as an air raid patrol centre.

8 Wembley. Between 14 and 24 June 1924 it was the venue for the First International Cowboy (Rodeo) Championships.

9 Wembley. The appearances in question were those in FA Cup Finals (3 wins and 3 defeats) and season-opening Charity Shield matches (9 wins, 3 defeats), 4 League Cup Finals (4 wins and 2 defeats).

10 Highbury. It's supposed to be that of Herbert Chapman, the great Arsenal manager who died of pneumonia.

Gruesome Grounds

Do you play football? Then the chances are that you've played on some foul pitches – you know, the sorts that make you think they were once a camel's graveyard. Or perhaps you've had to get changed in some even fouler dressing rooms – the kind with last year's mud on the floor and showers which do more dribbling than most wingers. Well that's the way it was for most professional players in the early days. In fact, it was like that for some of them in the not-so-early days...

I've got a sinking feeling!

In December 1961, Watford were playing Grimsby Town in an old Third Division match at their Vicarage Road ground. Playing for Watford was an ex-Tottenham Hotspur player named Tommy Harmer. Harmer was very short, just 5ft 6in (1m 67cm), but so skilful that his lack of inches had never been a problem – at least, not until that day. Then Watford won a free kick out on the right wing. Harmer ran across to take it ... only to begin disappearing down a gaping hole that had suddenly appeared in the ground!

What did Harmer say afterwards?

a) "I thought I was going to be buried alive!"

b) "It was a hole new ball game today!"

c) "I think Watford should change their name to Hole City!"

The cause of the trouble was that the ground was built on the site of an old quarry. Torrential rain the night before had soaked in to that part of the pitch and Harmer's weight had been enough to make it subside.

Was the game abandoned? No, it was just delayed while the groundsman filled the hole with several buckets of sand and then covered it with bits of grass dug from the surrounds of the pitch.

What a shower!

Top Argentinian club River Plate sailed to various home grounds before ending up at their present stadium, the Monumental. One of them was in the Sarandi area of Buenos Aires, in 1906. By now a reasonably well-established club, River Plate decided for the first time in their history, to have their own stadium built.

When the day came for it to be officially checked out by a Football Association inspector, though, one big problem still remained – a total lack of a working water system. None of the pipework had been connected. All the club officials could hope was that the inspector would see the pipes and not bother to check any further.

They were out of luck. When he reached the changing rooms the inspector decided to test the showers. As he reached for a tap the officials showing him round turned away in embarrassment – only to turn back in amazement as a stream of water began gushing out! They were still reeling with shock when the satisfied inspector told them the ground had passed its inspection and left.

Had the water system suddenly been installed? Not

quite. On the other side of the changing room wall two of the club's founders, Enrique Salvarezza and Alfredo Zanni, had set up some ramshackle piping leading to the back of the showers. When they'd heard the tap being turned on they'd pumped buckets of water into it and hoped the inspector was a bit of a drip!

THE BRICKLAYING MANAGERS AWARD...

Bob Paisley (Liverpool). Paisley was a Liverpool player who became a brilliantly successful Liverpool manager (1974–83), leading his team to 13 major trophies. Before turning professional, though, Paisley had been a bricklayer by trade. When he joined Liverpool in 1939 one of his first jobs was to help build the Anfield brick dug-out where he'd later sit as manager.

Playing with style

Clever thinking goes down just as well at village football level. After their pitch was dug up by a herd of wild pigs in 2002, the footballers in the Dutch village of Putbroek came up with a stylish solution to ensure that it didn't happen again. They covered their pitch with ... human hair! According to a local farmer: "Pigs have a very well developed sense of smell. As soon as they catch a human smell they run away, never to return."

Stadium Stumpers

Every top team needs a top stadium to play in; and every top stadium needs a name to remember. For instance, everybody knows that Manchester United play at Old Trafford. But what does the word "Trafford" mean?

a) Theatre with a dream.

b) Area known for cream.

c) Valley with a stream.

Answer:
c) It's thought that "Trafford" comes from the two words "trough" and "ford", meaning a spot in a valley (trough) where you could cross (ford) a stream.

Here's a quiz about some other top stadiums. Match the name of the stadium with the correct explanation of what its name means.

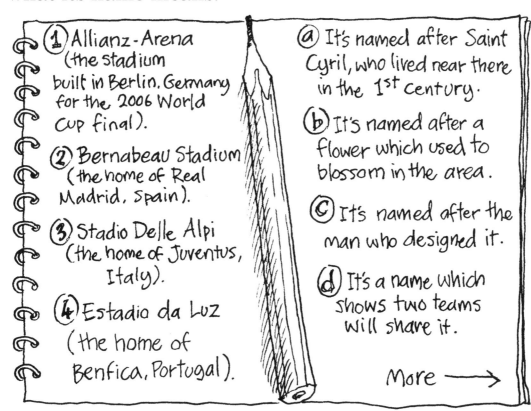

① Allianz-Arena (the stadium built in Berlin, Germany for the 2006 World Cup final).

② Bernabeau Stadium (the home of Real Madrid, Spain).

③ Stadio Delle Alpi (the home of Juventus, Italy).

④ Estadio da Luz (the home of Benfica, Portugal).

ⓐ It's named after Saint Cyril, who lived near there in the 1st century.

ⓑ It's named after a flower which used to blossom in the area.

ⓒ It's named after the man who designed it.

ⓓ It's a name which shows two teams will share it.

More ⟶

⑤ Etadio Azteca (the joint home of Cruz Azul and Necaxa, Mexico).

⑥ Hanappi Stadion (the home of Rapid Vienna. Austria).

⑦ Miyagi Stadium (used in 2002 World Cup, Japan).

⑧ Nou Camp (home of Barcelona, Spain).

⑨ San Siro (home of AC Milan and Inter Milan. Itay).

ⓔ The most boring name in world football. It means "new ground"!

ⓕ It's named after an ex-player.

ⓖ It's a description of what it looks like when there's a night game.

ⓗ It means it's near some very big mountains.

ⓘ It's named after the country's most famous ancient people.

Answers:

1d) After the 2006 World Cup the stadium became the joint home (hence "alliance" arena) of the German clubs Bayern Munich and TSV Munich 1860.

2f) Santiago Bernabeu was a star Real Madrid player. After retiring he became club President and was in charge when the stadium that bears his name was built.

THE SMOOTHEST, FLATTEST, LOP-SIDED PITCH AWARD...

The Bernabeu Stadium, Madrid.

When one Spanish newspaper tried to sum up how important a player Alfredo di Stefano had been to the five-time European Cup winners, Real Madrid, it wrote: "the pitch at the Santiago Bernabeu Stadium leans to the left because Alfredo Di Stéfano played so much on that side."

3h) The stadium's name means "Stage of the Alps" and mountains don't come too much bigger than that! Fittingly, the end of the ground used by Juventus's most loyal supporters is named after one of their most loyal players – Gaetano Scirea. Sporting Scirea, who wasn't once sent off or suspended in his long career, was travelling to look at possible new players for the club when he was killed in a car crash.

4g) It means "Stadium of Light" – a flashy place for a club who played their first-ever game on a patch of waste ground! The place got even flashier in 2004. It was rebuilt in time for the European Championships in Portugal.

5i) The only stadium to host two World Cup finals (in 1970 and 1986), it's named after the native Mexican people, the Aztecs – who, fittingly, were famous for the beauty of their architecture. It's strong, too. In 1985 it survived a terrible earthquake in Mexico City, which destroyed over 800 buildings.

6c) Gerhard wasn't just a top player with Austria's top club, he was also a fully qualified architect. So whereas most players just haunt stadiums when they retire, handy Hanappi was able to design a new one for Rapid. When he died, the stadium was named after him.

7b) The Miyagi stadium is named after the Miyagi area in which it's situated ... and the area is named after the beautiful purplish-red or white miyagi bush clover blossoms, which flourish there every autumn.

8e) Needless to say, Barcelona moved there from their "old ground" in 1957. Before that they'd played in all sorts of dodgy spots, from a park to a place called Hotel Casanovas. Maybe that's why one of the first things they did was have the ground blessed by the Archbishop of Barcelona.

9a) Both the Milan teams, Inter and AC, now share the ground, although when opened in 1926 it was Inter's ground alone. The name San Siro comes from the area in which it's situated and it's still the name by which the stadium is known throughout the world. Officially, though, it's the Guiseppe Meazza stadium. Meazza played 408 games (and scored 287 goals) for Inter and was a World Cup winner with Italy in 1934 and 1938. When he died in 1979 the decision was taken to name the ground in his honour – although whether Joseph Guiseppe is a nicer name than Cyril is a matter of taste!

Derby Ding-Dongs

"Derby" matches are fans' favourites. Why, what's so special about them? Well, funnily enough, it's nothing to do with how good the two teams are. Sometimes they're equally good, but they can just as well be equally bad. Neither does it matter if the teams are badly matched. One of them can be full of ball-balancing brilliance while the other is full of ball-battering badness. What matters in a Derby match is that it's between two teams whose grounds are very close together. This means that the fans live very close together, too – which means that the supporters of the winners will be able to taunt the fans of the losers every day of the week until the next Derby match comes around.

Two teams whose grounds couldn't get any closer are the Italian clubs Internazionale and AC Milan. That's because, as we've seen, they share the same ground – the San Siro Stadium. In 2003 it was the scene of the most peculiar victory ever seen in the European Champions Cup. Inter Milan and AC Milan had been drawn against each other in the semi-finals – so the first problem the two teams had to resolve was which of them was playing at "home" and which was playing "away" for each leg of the two-legged match. That's when it all got totally weird. With AC at "home", the first match was drawn 0–0. The second leg was also a draw, 1–1. But as AC Milan were now the "away" team, their goal was classed as an "away" goal and counted double. They went on to the final and won!

Derby games began in – come on, you should be able to guess by now – England! But in which English town was the first Derby match played?

a) Derby

b) Nottingham

c) Portsmouth

Answer:

b) Notts (for Nottingham) County are the oldest league football club in the world. They were founded in 1862, with neighbours Nottingham Forest following along in 1865 to become the third oldest club in the world. The two teams played each other for the first time a year later, in 1866. Sure enough, the match was marked by a dispute. According to Nottingham Forest's official history, they won the match 1–0 ... but a local newspaper report the morning after the game said it was a 0–0 draw!

So why aren't Derby matches called "Nottingham" games? Because of yet another Englishman: a very posh one, the Earl of Derby. Not because he was a footballer, though; he wasn't. The enterprising Earl was a horse-racing fan and, way back in 1780, he founded just about the most famous horse race in the world: the Derby. (It's still being run – but not by the same horses, of course!) As the popularity of the race grew, so contests between near-neighbours began to be called "local Derbies".

Now every big football city or town has teams whose meetings are called "Derby matches" – and if you're looking for arguments and punch-ups, you won't find matches that are much worse. Compare the disputed score of that first Nottingham Derby with this collection and ask yourself: whose Derby games are foul, and whose are even fouler?

The Manchester Derby: Manchester United v Manchester City

The 1974 match between the two Manchester teams ended up with nobody left on the pitch! After a fight, referee Clive Thomas sent off both United's Lou Macari and City's Mike Doyle. When they refused to go, Thomas came up with a clever scheme – he took all the other players off the field instead! Macari and Doyle had no choice but to follow them. Crafty Clive then brought everybody beside Macari and Doyle back again to finish the match!

The Milan Derby: Internazionale v AC Milan

Inter fans have the one thing a supporter wants – a  taunt that can't be answered. In their case it's a chant of "Serie B" (B-league)! In 1979 AC Milan were found guilty of match-fixing and forcibly relegated. They bounced back up again but two years later were relegated once more, this time because they were hopeless. So why is it such an unanswerable taunt? Because, unlike their rivals, Inter have never been relegated.

The Buenos Aires Derby: Boca Juniors v River Plate

The teams who share Argentina's capital city have been rivals since River Plate moved away from the dockland area where both began to set up anew in a much smarter area. Since then, Boca Juniors have been known as the "workers' team" and River Plate the "snobs' team".

While the teams are battling it out, the fans like to call each other names. To bawling Boca fans, River Plate are "chickens" – that is, scared of them. It dates back to the 1980s when they probably were: at that time Boca had the world star Diego Maradona in their team and won the Derby games every time! As for the roaring River Plate fans, their foul name for Boca is "pig". In fact, it's even fouler than that. The Spanish word for pigs is "bosteros", a word that comes from "bosta", meaning horse dung!

THE WETTEST RIVALRY AWARD...
Portsmouth and Southampton.
These two English teams meet in what they call the South Coast derby. Portsmouth proudly claim that they're the home of the Royal Navy. Southampton answer that they're the cruise ship capital of the world – to which Pompey fans like to reply, "Yeah – it's where the Titanic set sail from!"

The Glasgow Derby: Celtic v Rangers
The two Scottish clubs have a long history of both fabulous football and foul fights but on 17 October 1987 they were shown how to be even fouler – by two English internationals. Chris Woods, Rangers' goalkeeper, was sent off for punching Celtic's striker Frank McAvennie (who was also sent off for striking back!). He was followed by defender Terry Butcher, who put through

his own goal, then followed up by trying to put Celtic's goalkeeper through *his* own goal.

Sherriff Archibald McKay, a Glasgow magistrate, showed that – unlike the players – he wasn't a fan of foul football. Butcher and Woods were both found guilty of a breach of the peace and fined.

The Montevideo Derby: Nacional v Penarol

But for foul Derby encounters, the Uruguayan teams Nacional and Penarol must be hard to beat. They were bad enough in 1990 when a massive fight broke out during their Derby game – and the referee set a record by dishing out red cards to 21 of the 22 players!

But in 2000, the sides hit an even fouler level. At the end of a bad-tempered 1–1 draw another brawl broke out. This time the police moved in with red cards of their own. Six punching Penarol players and three nasty Nacional men were arrested and thrown into jail for a week. They were only let out after promising to behave better in the future, and telling Uruguay's Ministry of Sport and Youth that they'd agree to give some free coaching to children.

So, have you made your mind up? Is football a fouler

game today than it was when it first began to spread across the world?

Perhaps the answer is: sometimes.

What we all hope, though, is that football doesn't become even fouler as a result of players believing that winning is all that matters. It isn't. Football's a fantastic game, but that's all it is: a game about scoring more goals and having fun.

Let's end with the words of Alfredo di Stefano, who played in South America and Europe, and scored over 800 goals in stadiums around the world:

A soccer game without goals is like an afternoon without sunshine.

So have fun – and may the sun shine on all your football matches (especially at the other team's end!).

FOUL FOOTIE QUIZ

INTRODUCTION

Football is full of facts. Some are foul, some are fantastic – and, let's face it, some are fiendishly difficult. The trouble is, it always seems to be the fiendishly difficult ones that other fanatical fans (like your mates) ask you questions about…

Because professional football has been played for well over a hundred years, they'll boringly bombard you with deadly dates as well:

If you know a fan like that then … congratulations! Because the Foul Footie Quiz is going to give you a chance to hit back with questions they won't be able to answer – questions about the foul and fascinating facts that make football such a glorious game!

Scary questions like:

or low-down questions like:

So if you want to discover the funniest football facts, read on! They're foul!

FOUL FOOTBALL HISTORY

1 Here's an easy question to start you off with. What did the nineteenth-century playwright Oscar Wilde say about football? Just fill in the gaps in this quotation:

FOOTBALL IS ALL VERY WELL AS A GAME FOR ROUGH (a) .... BUT IT'S HARDLY SUITABLE FOR DELICATE (b) ....

(Clue: the two missing words are *boys* and *girls*)

Answer:
1 a – girls; b – boys. (He was being funny.)

Rough rules

Fouls in football are what you call breaking the rules. But what are the rules of football? They've changed a bit since Oscar Wilde's time.

See if you can sort out the fair from the foul in this collection...

2 It's 1878. A player takes a throw-in with one hand. **Fair or foul?**

3 It's 1888. A goalkeeper is about to save a shot when suddenly he's charged over by one of the other team with the result that the ball sails into the goal. **Fair or foul?**

4 It's 1892. The ball is passed back to the goalkeeper and he picks it up. **Fair or foul?**

5 It's 1902. A player runs out on to the pitch and you can see his knees. **Fair or foul?**

6 It's 1907. A goalkeeper dives off his line before a penalty is taken. **Fair or foul?**

7 It's 1908. The goalkeeper again. This one catches the ball way outside his penalty area, bounces it a few hundred times as he charges up to near the halfway line, then takes a shot at the opposition's goal. **Fair or foul?**

8 It's 1920. A player scores direct from a corner. **Fair or foul?**

Answers:

2 Fair. The two-hands rule was introduced in the 1880s, because some players were able to hurl the ball miles with one hand.

3 Fair. Charging a goalkeeper, even when he didn't have the ball, was allowed until 1890.

4 Fair. This didn't become a foul for another 100 years!

5 Foul. Until 1904 there was a Football Association rule saying that shorts had to reach below a player's knees.

6 Foul. It was allowed until 1905 … and it's been allowed since 1997! In between, it wasn't.

7 Fair. Until 1912 a goalkeeper could catch the ball anywhere in his own half. One of the players who caused the rule to be changed was Portsmouth's Matthew Reilly. He'd played Gaelic football in Ireland (in which players can run with the ball while they're bouncing it) and once he caught the ball, nobody could get it off him!

8 Foul. This wasn't allowed until 1924.

Football firsts

Every football feature was first featured sometime. Can you work out which of these pairs of football features was featured in football first?

Answers:

9–b) The referee's whistle was first heard in 1878, on Notts Forest's ground. Shirt numbers didn't arrive in the football league until 60 years later, in 1939, when both Arsenal and Chelsea wore them in league games.

10–a) Although goalkeepers were known as "net-minders" for a while, the term goalkeeper was used from around 1870 – it had to be, goal nets weren't invented until 1891! Special goalkeepers' jerseys arrived in 1908; until then goalkeepers had worn the same shirts as the rest of their team – very confusing!

11–a) A Nottingham Forest player, Sam Widdowson, invented shinguards in 1874. But heads were thought more valuable than shins – for the first five seasons of the Football League, until 1893, heading the ball was banned.

12–b) The word "soccer" was first used in 1889. White footballs didn't appear in league matches until 1951!

FOUL FOOTBALL CLUBS

'Orrible origins

Football is an eleven-a-side team game – which means that if you want to play the game properly the first thing you've got to find is another ten players to join you.

That's exactly how most of today's big-name football clubs got started. They were formed by groups of old school friends or work-mates or whoever, deciding that they wanted to play this new-fangled game called football.

Match these names of clubs with their fascinating start-up facts: Celtic, Coventry City, FK Austria, Fulham, Juventus, Notts County, Leyton Orient, Sheffield Wednesday, Sunderland, West Ham.

13 They were formed by a group of teachers.

14 They were formed by shop-assistants who had to work all day every Saturday and could only play on their early closing day during the week.

15 They were formed by workers at a bicycle factory.

16 They started life as a church team.

17 They were formed in 1904 by a group of workers at the yard which built HMS Warrior, the first warship made with iron.

I KNOW IT WORKS FOR WARSHIPS, BUT...

18 They were formed as a cricket and football club in the 1890s by some Englishmen who'd gone to live in another country. The cricket didn't catch on, but the football did!

19 They were formed in 1897 by a group of students.

20 They were formed in 1888 by two local businessmen and a Catholic priest named Brother Wilfred. For the next 110 years Catholic priests were allowed in to watch their games free of charge!

21 They were formed in 1881 by desk-bound clerks of a shipping company.

22 They were formed in 1862, making them the world's oldest existing football league club. Their early games were against themselves – they had to be, there weren't any other teams to play!

Answers:

13 Sunderland – which is a shortened version of their first name: The Sunderland and District Teachers Association FC!

14 Sheffield Wednesday – although their first name was simply The Wednesday because that was the day of the week they played on.

15 Coventry City – although their first name was Singers FC, after the name of the bicycle company they worked for.

16 Fulham – which is a shortened version of their first name, Fulham St Andrews Sunday School FC.

17 West Ham United – whose first name was Thames Ironworks FC.

18 FK Austria.

19 Juventus – who used to play in red until one of their players came over to England, saw Notts County in their black-and-white stripes, and liked them so much he went back to Italy and talked his team into changing their colours!

20 Celtic.

21 Leyton Orient – although their first name was simply Orient FC, after the shipping company the clerks worked for.

22 Notts County – who are also the most relegated side in the British Football League!

Cool colours

What colours should your team wear? That's a problem all clubs have faced. Sometimes they've done it the easy way and copied another club's colours. For example:

• In the 1960s Leeds United changed from a strip of yellow and blue to all white because they were the colours of Real Madrid, the then European Champions, and their manager Don Revie thought it might inspire them to play the same way!

• They were only doing what Tottenham Hotspur did years before. They switched to white shirts and blue shorts in 1899, the year they decided they wanted to look like the top team of that era, Preston North End.

Try these questions on team strips – but don't get shirty if you don't know the answers!

23 Arsenal's shirts are now red and white, but until 1933 only one of those colours featured in their strip. Which one?

278

24 What don't top Spanish club Barcelona have on their shirts that every other top European side do have?

25 British teams Barnet, Blackpool, Hull, Motherwell, Dundee United and Wolves all play in orange shirts – but what else do they have in common?

26 In 1883, before they switched to plain white, Bolton Wanderers wore white shirts with – what?

27 Everton's first shirts were black with a white stripe; but where did the stripe start, and where did it end?

Answers:

23 Red – the same colour as Nottingham Forest. Why? Because Arsenal's first ever set of football shirts were given to them … by Nottingham Forest.

24 The name of a sponsor. They think one would spoil the look of their famous blue and red striped shirts.

25 None of them say their shirts are orange. Wolves say they're "gold"; Blackpool and Dundee United say they're "tangerine"; Barnet, Motherwell and Hull say they're "amber".

26 Red spots! They didn't think it made their players look like they'd caught the measles, they thought they made them look bigger and beefier.

27 They had a white sash, which started at one shoulder and crossed to the opposite waist.

FOUL FOOTBALL MATCHES

Competition quandaries

In the early days, football matches were always friendly matches (even when they were foul friendlies). Then league and cup competitions began. Now almost every country in the world has its own football league and cup competitions. On top of those, there are competitions between clubs in different countries. On top of those, there are international competitions between countries themselves. And on top of those ... well, there aren't any competitions on top of those yet – but if life's ever discovered anywhere else in the universe then an Inter-planetary Cup won't be far behind.

YOU'LL HAVE TO GET ON THE SPACE SHUTTLE, MR BERGKAMP

NO THANKS, I'LL WALK

28 When were these ten club football competitions first won? Put them into order, oldest first.

(a) THE ENGLISH FOOTBALL LEAGUE
(b) THE EUROPEAN CHAMPIONS CUP
(c) THE SOUTH AMERICAN CLUB CUP
(d) THE FA CUP
(e) THE FA PREMIER LEAGUE
(f) THE SCOTTISH FOOTBALL LEAGUE
(g) THE UEFA CUP
(h) THE SCOTTISH FA CUP
(i) THE LEAGUE OF WALES
(j) THE AFRICAN CHAMPIONS CUP

Answer:
28 d) (1872), **f)** (1874), **a)** (1888), **f)** (1891), **b)** (1956), **g)**
(1958), **c)** (1960), **j)** (1975), **e)** (1993), **i)** (1993)

The phenomenal FA Cup

The English FA Cup has seen so many phenomenal games you could write a whole book about it. (Actually, somebody has! Me! It's called The Phenomenal FA Cup.) Some parts of the Cup's history are so phenomenal they make you wonder if they're really true...

Which of the following are phenomenal FA Cup facts, and which are foul fibs?

29 A team called The Wanderers once reached the FA Cup Final without playing a match. **True or false?**

30 A player named William Harrison had two reasons to celebrate in 1908. One the same day his team, Wolverhampton Wanderers, won the Cup and his wife gave birth to twins. **True or false?**

31 In the 1946 FA Cup Final a player named Jack Stamp stamped on the ball and it burst. True or false?

32 The FA Cup has never been won by a non-league team. **True or false?**

33 A team once played in the FA Cup Final after being beaten in an earlier round. **True or false?**

34 At the end of one Wembley final, the Cup was presented to somebody who hadn't even played in the match. **True or false?**

35 In one FA Cup tie, a Manchester United player spent the last 20 minutes of the game trying not to score. **True or false?**

36 Bert Turner (Charlton, 1946), Tommy Hutchison (Manchester City, 1981) and Gary Mabbutt (Tottenham Hotspur, 1987) all scored for their own team and for the opposition in FA Cup Finals and their teams still won the match. **True or false?**

Answers:

29 True. Wanderers were the Cup holders, having won the first-ever competition in 1872. The next season they were allowed to go straight to the Final. The rule was abolished after that.

30 False. Harrison did win with Wolves, but it was his wife who scored a hat trick – she gave birth to triplets, not twins!

31 False. The ball burst as Stamp took a shot. He didn't care. He scored twice and his team, Derby, beat Charlton 4-1.

32 False. When Tottenham Hotspur won in 1901 they were in the Southern League.

33 True. In 1945–46 ties up to (not including) the semi-finals were played over two legs, the only season it's happened. Charlton lost to Fulham in their third round first-leg game but won the tie on aggregate.

34 True. At the end of the 2000 Final, Chelsea captain Dennis Wise carried his baby son up with him when he collected the trophy. Not very wise. He might have dropped one of them.

THAT'S SOLVED THAT PROBLEM

35 True. Manchester United were beating Northampton Town 8-2 and their winger George Best had scored six of them. He said afterwards: "I was so embarrassed I played the last 20 minutes at left back."

36 False. All three players did score for both teams in each Final – but their own teams lost.

The legendary league

The Football League began in 1888–89 with just one division. In 1892–93 a second division was added. A third division came along in 1920–21, and a fourth division in 1921–22.

37 What didn't arrive until 1898–99, six years after the Second Division had been formed?

Answer:
37 Automatic relegation and promotion, in which bottom teams drop down and top teams in the division below go up to take their place.

In other words, the football league has seen its ups and downs! Will you be a promotion candidate or doomed to relegation in this legendary league quiz?

38 In 1996–97 Middlesbrough earned sufficient points to stay in the Premier League but still got relegated. **True or false?**

39 In happier times Middlesbrough, needing just one win to become champions of the old Second Division, were leading 1-0 against Luton Town. What did their manager, Jack Charlton, yell at the players near the end?

(a) LET THEM SCORE! (b) WE'RE THE CHAMPS! (c) YOU'RE ALL USELESS!

40 In 1990, Sunderland lost the old Second Division play-off final and yet they were still promoted. **True or false?**

41 Every season between 1921–22 and 1926–27, Plymouth Argyle came second in their division but weren't promoted once. Why not?

a) Teams wouldn't travel as far as Devon.

b) They lost six play-off matches in a row.

c) Only one team could win promotion.

42 Nowadays the champions of the Football Conference League are promoted to the Football League's Third Division to take the place of the bottom club. But in 1996 the Conference champions Stevenage Borough were told they had to stay where they were because they weren't good enough. **True or false?**

43 On one Saturday, in January 1965, the whole football league programme was cancelled because of what?

a) Bad weather.

b) A funeral.

a) A referee's strike.

...WE SHALL NOT, WE SHALL NOT, WE SHALL NOT BE MOVED...

44 The lowest attendance for a league match was recorded when Leicester City played Stockport County on the last day of the 1920–21 season. Just 130 spectators turned up. True or false?

45 The city of Liverpool's two teams, Everton and Liverpool, were both unhappy when Liverpool were relegated from the old First Division in 1954 because they wouldn't be playing against each other. How did they get round the problem?

a) They played a special floodlit friendly match every year.

b) They invented their own competition.

c) They played each other at tiddlywinks instead.

FOUL, REF!

PING!

Answers:

38 True. What pushed them into the relegation zone was having three points deducted for not turning up for a match.

39 a) Middlesbrough were playing away and Charlton really wanted to win the league in front of their home crowd – so he encouraged his players to turn a win into a draw! They disobeyed him, and became champions that day.

40 True. They took the place of Swindon Town who, even though they'd gained enough points to stay up, were relegated from the top division as a punishment for making illegal payments.

41 c) Plymouth were in the (very old) Third Division which was divided into Northern and Southern sections and only the top team in each section won promotion to the Second Division.

42 False. It was the Stevenage ground that wasn't good enough.

43 b) The war-time Prime Minister, Sir Winston Churchill, was given a State Funeral so the whole country stopped.

44 False. It was worse than that. The match was played at Old Trafford, miles from either Leicester or Stockport, so only 13 fans watched the match!

45 a) and **b)** The two clubs invented their own competition, The Floodlit Challenge Cup which was a sort of serious-friendly match. It was scrapped in 1963. Why? Because that's when Liverpool were promoted and the two clubs started meeting in the league again.

Mad matches

The best football matches of all are those where you just don't know what's going to happen next – like in these mad matches…

The scene is set. The build-up is big. The action is awesome. But the finish is missing. Can you use your skill and judgement to work out what happened next?

46 It's 6th March, 1875. England are due to face Scotland in an international match at the Kennington Oval in London. Kick-off time arrives – but England's goalkeeper Bill Carr doesn't. He's been delayed… *What happened next?* (Clue: "Come on, the ten men!")

47 It's April 1977, and Derby County are playing Manchester City. The referee's whistle shrieks – and, soon after, a groundsman is running on to the pitch with a paintbrush in his hand… *What happened next?* (Clue: he wasn't penalized)

PERHAPS SOMEONE NEEDS TO BRUSH UP ON HIS SKILLS!

48 It's Wimbledon v Liverpool. Wimbledon win a corner and their man Neil Ardley runs over to take it. He places the ball next to the corner flag, steps back, runs in and… *What happened next?* (Clue: it was certainly a corner kick!)

49 It's 1931, and Chelsea are playing at Blackpool in pouring rain on a freezing cold afternoon. The 6,000 crowd begin yelling "Southern Softies" as a Chelsea player starts shivering with cold. *What happened next?* (Clue: it could be why Chelsea's nickname is "The Blues")

50 It's New Year's Day in 1966, and Chester are playing a Fourth Division match against Aldershot when one of their full-backs, named Jones, breaks his leg. His partner at full-back – another Jones, but no relation – offers his sympathy, then gets back to the match. *What happened next?* (Clue: it was a cracking game – for all the wrong reasons)

51 It's the 1995-96 season. Leeds United's Gary McAllister, playing against Chelsea, chases after a ball which is going out of play. Unable to stop, McAllister tumbles over the boards surrounding the pitch and lands right in the lap of a Chelsea fan. *What happened next?* (Clue: up for the cup!)

ER... COME ON, CHELSEA!

52 It's 1996 and Bolton Wanderers are leading 1-0 against Reading, thanks to a goal by their striker, John McGinlay. Then Bolton's goalkeeper Keith Branagan is sent off and McGinlay takes his place between the posts. *What happened next?* (Clue: not a lot)

And, finally, a what happened before question.

53 It's 1986, and Fulham are preparing to meet Liverpool in the second leg of a League Cup tie. Fans who arrive for the match and buy their programme are amused to discover details about what will happen if the two teams are tied on aggregate at the end of the match. Why? *What happened before?* (Clue: double trouble)

Answers:

46 England started the game without a goalkeeper at all! Carr finally arrived – and let in two goals as the teams drew 2-2. Perhaps England should have played the whole game without him: against the ten men Scotland hadn't scored!

47 The groundsman painted a new penalty spot at one end of the pitch. The referee had just awarded a penalty – only to find that the penalty spot had disappeared!

48 Ardley kicked the corner flag and missed the ball altogether.

49 The frozen Chelsea player left the pitch and didn't return. So, one by one, did four more of his Southern softy team-mates! Chelsea ended the game with six players on the field and lost 4-0.

50 Jones number two broke his leg as well.

51 The Chelsea fan tipped his cup of coffee down the front of McAllister's shirt after giving the Leeds player a piece of his mind.

52 McGinlay didn't let a goal in to complete the remarkable feat of scoring the winner and keeping a clean sheet in the same match.

53 Fulham had lost the first leg game 10-0. Imagining that they could level the scores by beating Liverpool by the same amount was being a little optimistic!

Glorious goals and groanful goals

Goals make a football match. If your team score them, then you're deliriously happy. If the other team score them, then you're as miserable as the Newcastle fan who bought a "David Ginola" replica shirt … the day before the player left the club to go to Tottenham!

Of course you can still be pretty miserable even when your team do score – at least you can if it's at the wrong end. Own goals have been part of the game from the very beginning: the first official own goal in the football league was scored on the day the competition began in 1888.

Own goals are one of the fouler parts of football for both fan and player. Ask the Aston Villa fans who saw the amazing performance of their defender Chris Nicholl in a match against Leicester City in March, 1976. The final score was 2-2, with Nicholl scoring all four of the goals!

Can you sort out the good goals from the own goals? Each question describes a goal scored in a match. But was it a golden goal hammered into the right end – or a groanful goal thumped into the wrong end?

54 Liverpool v Blackburn, 1995. The ball trickled along the ground towards Blackburn's goalkeeper, Tim Flowers, hit a lump of grass ... and bounced into the net. **Golden or groanful?**

55 Charlton v Middlesbrough, 1960. High in the air, the ball came over from the wing. For some reason the Middlesborough goalkeeper, Peter Taylor, didn't jump ... and into the net it went. **Golden or groanful?**

56 Queens Park Rangers v Barnsley, 1997. From the edge of the penalty area, Trevor Sinclair of QPR kicked the ball over his head to score one of the most amazing goals the crowd had ever seen. **Golden or groanful?**

57 Manchester United v Liverpool, 1977. The ball whizzed into the penalty box. Manchester United's Jimmy Greenhoff tried to get out of the way – unsuccessfully. The ball hit him and spun into the net. **Golden or groanful?**

58 Nottingham Forest v Manchester City, 1990. City's goalkeeper Andy Dibble was gazing around, deciding what to do next, the ball balanced on the palm

289

of his hand. Seconds later it was in the net! **Golden or groanful?**

59 Leicester v Chelsea, 1954. Two Leicester players, Stan Milburn and Jack Froggatt, stretched for the ball. Both made contact at exactly the same instant – and whizzing into the goal it went. **Golden or groanful?**

60 Charlton Athletic v Derby County, 1992. Darren Pitcher of Charlton played a long ball from near the half-way line to his team-mate Scott Minto, prowling on the edge of the penalty area. Without letting the ball bounce, Minto scored with a fine header! **Golden or groanful?**

61 Liverpool v Wimbledon, 1988. In a furious goalmouth scramble, the ball was kicked off the Liverpool line only to be headed straight back into the net. **Golden or groanful?**

62 Fulham v Sheffield Wednesday, 1961. Fulham kicked off. They

played the ball coolly from man to man – until Fulham's captain Alan Mullery slid the ball into the net before a Sheffield player had even touched it! **Golden or groanful?**

63 Barrow v Plymouth Argyle, 1963. With the score at 0-0, Ivan Robinson put the ball into the net to give Barrow a 1-0 win … but he wasn't a Barrow player. **Golden or groanful?**

Answers:

54 Golden. It was a mis-hit shot by Stan Collymore of Liverpool; so bad, in fact, that Collymore turned away in disgust and missed seeing the ball go into the net!

55 Golden. The ball went into the net direct from a corner taken by Johnny Summers of Charlton, to make the score an amazing 6-6. And the reason the Middlesbrough goalkeeper didn't jump? Unseen by the referee, a Charlton player was standing on his foot!

56 Golden. Sinclair had let fly with a stunning bicycle kick.

57 Golden. Greenhoff had been trying to get out of the way of team-mate Lou Macari's shot – and so ended up accidentally scoring the winning goal in the 1977 FA Cup Final as Manchester United beat Liverpool 2-1.

58 Golden. While Dibble was dithering, Gary Crosby of Notts Forest headed it off his hand and popped it in the net. (It wasn't a foul, either. The rules say a goalkeeper has to have both hands on the ball before it's wrong to kick or head it out of them.)

59 Groanful. It was a joint own-goal (although they both probably felt quite half-hearted about admitting it!).

60 Groanful. Pitcher's pass was an accidental slice over his head, and Minto's contribution was an accidental header over his goalkeeper's head.

61 Groanful. The header was from Liverpool's goalkeeper Bruce Grobbelaar who'd been lying on the ground when the clearance hit him on the back of the nut!

62 Groanful. Fulham had been passing the ball backwards. Mullery finished the job off by passing it right back past his goalkeeper.

63 Golden. Because though Ivan Robinson wasn't a Barrow player, he wasn't an own-goal scoring member of Plymouth's team either. He was the referee! George McLean of Barrow had taken a long shot which was going wide until it hit Robinson and was deflected into the goal.

FOUL INTERNATIONAL FOOTBALL

International football, country versus country, is football at the highest level. World-class football. And so to be the manager of an international squad you've got to be able to talk...

World-class rhubarb

Replace the RHUBARBs in these statements from some England managers...

64 Sir Alf Ramsey, who took his team to the World Cup in 1970 said:

> *We have nothing to learn from the RHUBARB.*

65 Bobby Robson wasn't so sure. In 1988 he said: "*Maybe we're not as RHUBARB as we thought we were.*"

66 Things didn't go well for Graham Taylor. After his England team had let slip a one-goal lead to lose 2-1 to Sweden in 1992, he complained: "*We could have done with not having RHUBARB arriving, but you have to have RHUBARB.*"

67 Don Revie walked out on England in 1977, saying: "*I sat down with my wife and we agreed that the England job was no longer worth the RHUBARB.*"

68 But enthusiasm was Kevin Keegan's strong point, so let's give him the last word:

> *We can end the RHUBARB as it started – as the greatest football nation in the world!*

Still digging around for RHUBARB replacements? Here are the world-class words you need: *aggravation, Brazilians, good, half-time, millennium*

The Big Day

If you're a player, your big ambition will be to play for your country. However many times you manage it, you always hope you'll have a great game and that it will be a day to remember…

How did these international appearances work out? You decide!

69 GO Smith played centre-forward for England throughout the 1890s and was the first player to win 20 caps for his country. What did he refuse to do during games?
a) Foul an opponent.
b) Head the ball.
c) Help his defence.

70 Blackpool and England goalscorer Stan Mortensen played his first full international match in 1943. What was special about it?
a) He played in goal.
b) He played in a different colour shirt to the rest of the England team.
c) He played in borrowed boots.

COCO WAS THE ONLY PERSON WITH SPARE BOOTS!

71 Bill Nicholson played his first game for England against Portugal in 1951. What happened after just 19 seconds?

a) He scored for England.

b) He scored an own goal.

c) He was sent off.

72 Kevin Hector of Derby County first played for England in 1973. How long did his international career last?

a) 90 games.

b) 90 minutes.

c) 90 seconds.

Answers:

69 b) Smith believed that football was a game that should be played on the ground!

70 b) Because he played for Wales! Mortensen had been picked as a reserve and when Wales turned up short of players (which often happened with games during World War Two) Mortensen played for them instead.

71 a) It was his first touch in international football! Not surprisingly, Nicholson holds the record for the fastest goal scored by a player in his first match. More surprisingly, he also holds the record for the fastest goal scored by a player in his only international. Nicholson was never picked for England again!

72 c) Hector was thrown on as a last-gasp substitute with England desperately needing a goal against Poland to win a vital World Cup qualifying match. He scraped the post with a header, England went out of the competition and Hector didn't play for his country again.

Friend or foe?

An international match can be part of a competition, like the European Championships or the World Cup, or it can just be a "friendly" game.

Well, that's what internationals that aren't part of a competition are called…

Sort out the friendly from the unfriendly in this collection of international incidents.

73 It's 1968 and England have just arrived north of the border to play a friendly against Scotland. "Welcome to Scotland," says a journalist to the England manager, Sir Alf Ramsey. Is Ramsey's reply friendly or unfriendly?
74 It's 1936, and England are lining up to play Germany in Berlin. They've been told that when the German national anthem is played they should give the Nazi salute to avoid offending Germany's leader, Adolf Hitler, who is in the

crowd. Is the team's response friendly or unfriendly?

75 It's 1952, and France are playing Northern Ireland. Bonifaci, one of the French players, is injured and goes off for treatment. When he comes back to the pitch, what sort of welcome does he receive – friendly or unfriendly?

76 Between 1949 and 1957, how did Colombia treat other international sides? Were they friendly or unfriendly?

Answers:

73 Unfriendly. Ramsey replied, "You must be *@*£-ing joking!"

74 Friendly. Well, friendly in that they did give the Nazi salute. They then went on to give Germany a very unfriendly 6-3 beating!

75 Too friendly! The injured player was allowed back on, even though a substitute had already come on in his place. So France played with 12 men until the mistake was noticed at half-time.

DO YOU GET THE FEELING THEY HAVE MORE PLAYERS THAN US?

76 Unfriendly. Colombia had argued with the international Football Association, FIFA, and so didn't arrange a single international match during those eight years.

END-TO-END QUIZ

To finish with, here's a quiz to test your all-round knowledge of football. There are questions on clubs, players, goals – everything. They're all different. Except for one thing. They're all fiendishly foul!

77 Bristol Rovers were originally called by a very different name: *Purdown_____*. Fill in the gap.

a) PIRANHAS   b) POACHERS   c) PIRATES

78 TV viewers hoping to watch the highlights of the whole Celtic v Rangers Scottish League Cup Final in 1957–8 only got to see what happened in the first half. This was because the floodlights were too dim. **True or false?**

79 What did Luton Town ban from their home matches in 1986–87?

a) TV cameras.

b) Marching bands.

c) Away team supporters.

80 Barnsley FC were founded in 1888, when they bought their first ground. The man they bought it from laid down a strict condition, saying: "You have to_____. yourselves." Fill in the gap.

a) Behave.

b) Mow it.

c) Wash.

81 In their early days, Grimsby Town's players changed in workmen's huts. **True or false?**

82 When Manchester United arrived in Turkey to play Galatasaray in the 1993–94 European Champions League, they were met by banners saying: *Welcome to* _____. Fill in the gap.

a) Turkey.

b) Defeat.

c) Hell.

83 In 1995, Leyton Orient's ground at Brisbane Road was the first football stadium ever to be used for what?

84 In 1983 the USA launched a campaign for goalkeepers to wear what?

a) Helmets.

b) Shoulder pads.

c) Goggles.

85 In 1901, Liverpool advertised for new players in the sports newspaper Athletic News. **True or false?**

86 In 1970, West Ham's Bobby Moore pulled out of playing in a pre-season friendly because crooks had threatened to kidnap him. **True or false?**

87 In 1881, Sunderland had hardly any money in the bank. They were saved from going bust by one of their supporters selling his prize what?

a) Canary.

b) Red and white roses.

c) Vegetables.

88 Argentinian teams Nacional and Penarol were playing in 1932 when a Nacional shot whizzed outside the Penarol post. What happened next?

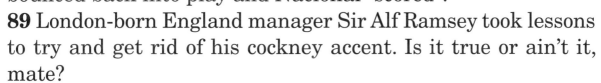

a) The ball flattened a spectator, who then started a riot.

b) The ball hit a soldier's rifle, causing it to go off and plug a hole in the Penarol goalie's cap.

c) The ball hit a cameraman's case, bounced back into play and Nacional "scored".

89 London-born England manager Sir Alf Ramsey took lessons to try and get rid of his cockney accent. Is it true or ain't it, mate?

90 Ian Rush was in the Liverpool team that played Arsenal in the 1987 League Cup Final. He scored, but Liverpool lost 2-1. What was unusual about that?

a) Rush was Liverpool's goalkeeper.

b) Until then, Liverpool had always won if Rush scored.

c) Exactly the same thing had happened the year before.

91 In the 1986 World Cup Finals, England's Ray Wilkins was sent off for throwing the ball to the referee. **True or false?**

92 What did the 1874, 1878, 1879, 1880 and 1881 FA Cup Finals have in common?

a) One of the teams hadn't had to play a semi-final match.

b) They were all won by the same team.

b) The winning team had lost the year before.

93 Cameroon star Roger Milla started a fashion with his goal celebration. What was it?

A FULL LENGTH DIVE   A WIGGLE AROUND THE CORNER FLAG   A HANDSTAND

94 In an unusual match between Belgian league teams AA Gent and Lokeren in 1994, a penalty was saved by a non-goalkeeper and scored by a goalkeeper. **True or false?**

95 When the FA appointed Don Revie as England manager Alan Hardaker, the boss of the Football League, said, "*You must be _____.*" What are the missing words?

a) *off your heads.*

b) *paying him a fortune.*

c) *really desperate.*

96 After a fight during the 1985 Bulgarian Cup Final, top player Hristo Stoichkov was banned for six months. **True or false?**

97 A goal by Holland's Rob Rensenbrink in 1978 reached a landmark in the history of the World Cup competition. Was it:

a) The 100th goal.

b) The 1,000th goal.

c) The 10,000th goal.

98 In December 2000 the Notts County players had to dodge some unusual creatures on their pitch. What were they?

DEAD FISH   VULTURES   POT-BELLIED PIGS

99 In 1871 it would have been legal to play a match with a football that was as big as a pumpkin or as small as an orange. **True or false?**

THIS ISN'T GOING TO WORK

100 In 1998 when Thailand met Indonesia in an Asian Tiger Cup game, Thailand won 3-2 with a goal in the last minute. What was unusual about it?

a) It went in off a wild dog that had run on to the pitch.

b) It was scored by the oldest international goalscorer ever.

c) It was a deliberate own-goal.

Answers:

77 b) They only ended as Bristol Rovers after another, double, change: to black shirts and the name Black Arabs!

78 False. It was the TV cameraman who was too dim. He forgot to take the lens-cap off the camera and the whole second-half recording was lost! (Probably just as well for the Rangers fans: Celtic had won the game 7-1!)

79 c) It was their way of stopping crowd trouble, but all it did was get them into trouble. They were thrown out of the League Cup competition because of it.

80 a) Barnsley must have done as he wanted because they've been there ever since!

81 False. The truth is even stranger. They changed in bathing huts wheeled up from a nearby beach!

82 c) It was, too. United were knocked out, had one player sent off and another couple belted by the Turkish police as they headed for the dressing room!

83 b) The ceremony was conducted by a Rev Alex Comfort – who just happened to be an ex-professional footballer.

84 a) Yes, they did know that the goalkeeper is the only player in the team who doesn't head the ball. They wanted to protect them from getting hurt diving at forwards' feet – but didn't think about what nasty injuries the helmets would cause those same feet!

85 True. It was a common thing to do in those days. The same edition also had "players wanted" ads from Sheffield Wednesday, Sheffield United, Preston and Southampton.

86 False. They'd threatened to kidnap his wife.

87 a) It raised £1, and that made all the difference. Besides, in those days £1 for a canary wasn't cheep!

88 c) The "goal" counted because the referee just wasn't snap-py enough to spot what had happened!

89 True, innit!

90 b) And as Rush had played his first game for Liverpool seven years before, and scored an awful lot of goals, that was an awful lot of winning games.

91 False. He was sent off for throwing the ball at the referee!

RIGHT! NOW I'M GOING TO THROW THE BOOK AT YOU!

92 a) In 1873, as holders, Wanderers went straight to the final. In the other seasons The Wanderers, Clapham Rovers (twice) and Old Etonians didn't have to play a semi-final because their opponents pulled out for different reasons.

93 b) Milla had cause to celebrate. At 42 years old, he's the oldest player to have scored in a World Cup finals match.

94 True. Eric Viscaal of AA Gent took over in goal when their keeper was sent off, saved a penalty with his first touch, then scored one at the other end to win the game.

95 a) Obviously, Hardaker didn't think Revie would do well … and he was right.

96 False *and* **true.** He was originally banned for life – but because he was such an important player for Bulgaria it was decided that six months was a long enough ban after all!

97 b)

98 a) The pitch had been flooded after a tributary of the

River Trent burst its banks and the fish came with the water. When the water went the fish made a bad mistake and stayed behind.

99 True. Until 1872, the match ball could be any size the teams wanted.

Spot the Giant Ball...

100 c) With both of the teams already qualified for the semi-final it was a match neither wanted to win because it meant they'd play favourites Vietnam. So with a minute left, Indonesian defender Mursyid Effendi belted the ball into his own goal! It didn't help. Both of them lost their semi-finals. They were also fined and banned when the tournament was over!

Final score

That's it, full time. If you've been looking at the question numbers you'll realize you've been asked 100 questions all together. So, how did you get on?

Over 75	No question about it, you're a top scorer.
50–74	Excellent. More on target than over the bar.
25–49	Not bad. A bit of shooting practice needed.
0–24	Oh dear. What a foul performance!